Hannelore Gottschalk

Englisch

Units 40–51

Mitarbeit:
Joe Hambrook
Graham Pascoe

Fachliche Beratung:
Hanns Höfer

Dieser Band enthält das Arbeitsmaterial zu den vom Bayerischen Rundfunk produzierten Lehrsendungen »Englisch für Anfänger« *Units* 40–51.
Der gesamte Kurs ist in Originalfassung auch auf DVD lieferbar.
www.telekolleg-info.de

13. Auflage 2017
© 2017 BRmedia Service GmbH
Alle Rechte vorbehalten
Fotos: Raimund M. Maxsein und Süddeutscher Verlag, Bilderdienst (S. 109), beide München
Umschlaggestaltung: Beate C. Eberle, München
Zeichnungen: Reiner Stolte, München
Gesamtherstellung: Kessler Druck + Medien GmbH, Bobingen
ISBN 978-3-941282-04-9

VORWORT

Die vorliegende Veröffentlichung schließt mit den Units 40–51 den Englischkurs ab. Sie erreichen damit ein Niveau, das ungefähr dem mittleren Schulabschluß für Englisch entspricht. Das Kernstück jeder Unit ist auch in diesem vierten Teil des Kurses wieder die Geschichte. Die humorvollen, gelegentlich grotesken Spielszenen lassen trotz ihrer grammatikalischen Ausrichtung typisch englische und amerikanische Verhaltensformen erkennen. In den Dialogen steckt erneut eine Fülle von sorgfältig ausgewählten Aussagen und Redewendungen, die Sie selber beim aktiven Sprechen anwenden können. Zu einer wirklichen Vertiefung und Festigung Ihrer Englischkenntnisse gelangen Sie, wenn Sie frühere Units, auch solche aus den Bänden 1–3, wiederholen. Unterstreichen Sie sich Sätze, von denen Sie glauben, Sie werden sie einmal selber verwenden und sprechen Sie diese laut nach. (Beispiele: *Excuse me, can you tell me the way to...? Is this seat taken? Have a nice day! I'll ring you back. I'd like to speak to... Can I have a word with you? You're welcome. etc.*)

Auf dem Gebiet der Grammatik finden Sie in diesem Band einige Strukturen, die über die Umgangssprache hinausgehen, die aber in der Schriftsprache (Zeitungen, Bücher, Vorträge) häufig vorkommen, wie z. B. die satzverkürzenden Partizipformen in Unit 48 und 50. In einer Abschlußprüfung spielen diese Sprachelemente eine Rolle.

Auf die Lektüre narrativer Texte bereiten wir Sie durch die *summaries* vor, in denen das Geschehen der Spielszenen nacherzählt wird. Die *summaries* sind auch zur Übertragung ins Deutsche geeignet.

Weitere Lesetexte sind die landeskundlichen Einleitungen, die am Anfang jeder Unit stehen. Sie sollen Ihr Wissen um Land und Leute bereichern.

Wir hoffen, daß Sie nach dem Studium dieses vierten Bandes in der Lage sind, die sprachlichen Situationen mit englischsprechenden Gesprächspartnern gut zu bewältigen und wünschen Ihnen weiterhin viel Freude und Erfolg mit unserem Englischkurs.

Hannelore Gottschalk
Hanns Höfer

INHALTSVERZEICHNIS

Unit	Situation	strukturelle Lernziele	kommunikative Lernziele	Seite
40	**Washington D.C.**	– ing-Form (II) nach Verben wie *enjoy, mind, dislike* nach Verb + Präposition wie *apologise for* mit eigenem Subjekt wie *it's no use, it's no good, David forgetting to come* – ing-Form im Wechsel mit Infinitiv	– nach dem Weg fragen – sich für eine Störung entschuldigen – jdn. willkommen heißen – Erstaunen zeigen – Rückfragen stellen – jdn. für etwas interessieren – etwas definieren – Mutmaßungen anstellen	7
41	**Crime in the city**	– Verwendung von Singular und Plural	produktiv: – höfliche Redewendungen im amerikanischen Sprachgebrauch – einen Weg beschreiben – einen Rat erteilen – jdn. warnen – Instruktionen erteilen – auf Vor- und Nachteile hinweisen rezeptiv: – Verstehen von Kurznachrichten – Erfassen von Slangausdrücken	18
42	**On campus**	– indirekte Rede (I) einleitendes Verb in der Gegenwart – Fragesatz in der indirekten Rede	– die Aussage eines Dritten weitergeben – indirekte Fragen stellen – jdn. um eine Gefälligkeit bitten	28
43	**Rehearsal**	– indirekte Rede (II) einleitendes Verb in der Vergangenheit Zeitverschiebung – Befehle oder Aufforderungen in der indirekten Rede	– über Vergangenes in der indirekten Rede berichten – ein Telefongespräch wiedergeben – ein Kompliment aussprechen – Kritik üben – Mißfallen ausdrücken	38

Unit	Situation	strukturelle Lernziele	kommunikative Lernziele	Seite
44	**At the dentist's**	– Passiv (II) Verlaufsform des Passivs persönliches Passiv Passivbildung mit 2 Objekten	– jdn. warnen – Gewohnheiten ausdrücken – Angst, Befürchtung ausdrücken – sich einen Termin geben lassen – Empfindungen formulieren – jdm. gute Besserung wünschen	47
45	**The new sports car**	– ing-Form (III) nach Adjektiv + Präposition wie *afraid of, good at* nach Substantiv + Präposition wie *chance of, interest in* nach Präpositionen wie *without, by, instead of*	– einen Vorgang schildern – um Erlaubnis bitten – sich für ein Mißgeschick entschuldigen – Überraschung ausdrücken – seine Betroffenheit vorbringen	55
46	**Going on strike**	– Infinitiv mit und ohne *to* – Objekt- und Infinitivkonstruktion	– Notwendigkeit, Gleichgültigkeit, Unzufriedenheit ausdrücken – eine Sorge äußern – Vorbehalte machen – Zustimmung ausdrücken – Änderungsvorschläge machen	63
47	**Car maintenance**	– *have (make, let, get)* in der Bedeutung „lassen, veranlassen" – *do* und *make*	– Erstaunen ausdrücken – Absicht und Entschlossenheit äußern – eine Entscheidung fällen – einen Rat geben – eine Befürchtung äußern – Hilfe anbieten	73
48	**An accident**	– Partizipien – Partizipialsätze (I) anstelle von Kausalsätzen, Temporalsätzen Relativsätzen	– jdn. aufmuntern – Bedauern äußern – einen Vorgang beschreiben (auch schriftlich) – Rückfragen stellen	81

Unit	Situation	strukturelle Lernziele	kommunikative Lernziele	Seite
49	**The Darts Champion**	– Gradadverbien *terribly, extremely, very, very much, fairly, rather, pretty, quite* – Absichtssätze – Verbindungen mit *ever*	– eine Verzögerung ausdrücken und begründen – sich wegen einer Verspätung entschuldigen – einen Vorschlag machen – Bewunderung äußern – Anweisungen geben – Zuversicht äußern	90
50	**Breakfast Television**	– Partizipialsätze (II) unverbundenes Partizip	produktiv: – eine Wunschvorstellung ausdrücken – eine Enttäuschung ausdrücken – Möglichkeiten zur Wahl stellen – etwas begründen – etwas in Aussicht stellen schriftliche Kommunikation: – Abfassen eines Lebenslaufs	99
51	**How a car is made**	– Passiv (III) Wiederholung sämtlicher Passivformen	– einen technischen Vorgang beschreiben	107
Alphabetisches Wortschatzregister				116
Aussprachehilfen zu Eigennamen				121
Aussprachehilfen zu Orts- und Ländernamen				122
Erklärung der grammatischen Bezeichnungen				122
Schlüssel zu den Übungen				123

UNIT 40

THE CONSTITUTION

We the People of the United States, in order to form a more perfect Union, establish Justice, insure domestic Tranquility, provide for the common defence, promote the general Welfare, and secure the Blessings of Liberty to ourselves and our Posterity, do ordain and establish this Constitution for the United States of America.

[Article I and following sections of the Constitution shown in handwritten script]

(CB) Washington was planned and built as a capital city on a site chosen by George Washington himself. D.C. stands for District of Columbia. It's the seat of the US government.

The whole system of American government is based on the principles established in the Constitution and the Bill of Rights.

The Constitution divides the powers of the government into three branches – the Executive branch, headed by the President, the Legislative branch, which includes both Houses of Congress, the Senate and the House of Representatives, and the Judicial branch, which is headed by the Supreme Court.

The Constitution limits the powers of each branch and prevents any one branch from gaining too much power. The White House is the official residence of the President of the United States. The President is chosen in a national election for a four-year term of office. He may be re-elected for a second term. The two great political parties, the Democrats and the Republicans, nominate the Presidential candidates.

The Capitol is the meeting-place of the American parliament, known as Congress. It consists of the Senate and the House of Representatives. There are a hundred Senators, two from each of the fifty states. One third of the Senate is elected every two years for a six-year term.

The House of Representatives has 435 members, who are elected every two years. Both Houses of Congress can introduce new laws. The Judicial branch is headed by the Supreme Court. The Court decides whether laws passed by Congress and the President are in line with the Constitution. Each of the fifty states has its own government. The chief executive in each state is the Governor. His position is similar to that of the President in the Federal Government.

40 A Washington D.C.

(J = Jane, R = Russell, S = Senator Gatewater, P = Miss Pendlebury)

(Massachusetts Avenue in Washington D.C.)

J Where are we?
R We're on Massachusetts Avenue.
J No. It must be "K" Street. What do the street signs say?
R That one says "Ped X-ing".
   That doesn't mean anything.
J Yes, it does. It means "Pedestrian Crossing".
R It's no use trying to find your way with such a small map.
   We don't even know where we are.
J Yes, look, there's another sign – "H" Street.
R Ah, "H" Street.
   Good! Now, I'm going to walk from here to the National Portrait Gallery. I'm looking forward to seeing the pictures there.
J Aren't you getting tired?
   Is it really worth walking around Washington all day?
R I like sightseeing, and I prefer to walk. I hate going on buses.
J So do I. I prefer taking a taxi.
   And I'm going to take one now – to the Capitol.
R Ah, yes. You've got to interview a Senator.
J Senator Gatewater.
   I've got to be at the Senator's office in ten minutes.

(Senator's office)

S Yeah!
P Excuse me interrupting, Senator, but Miss Egan is here, from the London Weekend Chronicle.
S Show her in and bring us some tea.

(Jane comes in)

S Ah! Miss Egan. It's a pleasure to welcome you to Washington D.C. and to Capitol Hill.
J And it's a pleasure being here, Senator Gatewater. Thank you for giving me some of your time.
S You're welcome. I've been looking forward to giving an interview to such a charming lady.

The Capitol, Washington D.C.

(secretary comes in with tea and cookies)

S Thank you, Miss Pendlebury. And as of now, no more interruptions, please. We're busy. Have some tea, and a cookie.
J Cookie? I don't understand.
S This is a cookie!
J Oh, I see. A biscuit!
S Yes. A cookie! Take two.
J Er – thank you.
S I enjoy eating cookies. And they're very important politically.
J Really?
S Yes. The President – President Turpin – eats cookies – he insists on eating

S   them all day long. Sometimes they stop him from talking.
J   I see what you mean.
S   So everyone in Washington eats cookies. Well, everyone who needs the support of the President.
J   I don't mind eating them, but you see –
S   Young lady, there's no denying that cookies are important for the defense of freedom and the American way of life.
J   I'm pleased to hear that because my boy-friend makes biscuits – er – cookies.
S   You don't say! He manufactures cookies! Gee! Where is he? Is he here, in Washington?
J   Yes. He's busy sightseeing. By now he's probably touring the FBI building.
S   I insist on meeting him. He could be very valuable politically.
J   Why?
S   Because this is election year.
J   But you don't have Presidential elections this year, do you?
S   No. We elect the President every four years. But there are some elections every two years.
J   I'm afraid you'll have to explain.
S   I'd be delighted to explain, Miss Egan. And it's perhaps worth mentioning for the readers of your paper that I'm running for Governor of my State this year.
J   But you're a Senator.
S   You're not letting me explain! I've been in Congress for twelve years.

(secretary puts her head round the door)

P   I apologise for interrupting you, Mr Gatewater.
S   Miss Pendlebury, I asked you –
P   It's a Mr Russell Grant calling Miss Egan. He says he's lost –
S   What has he lost?
P   He hasn't lost anything, Senator. He's gotten lost somewhere in Washington.
J   That's my boy-friend, Senator.
S   Well, help him, Miss Pendlebury! See that he gets where he wants to go! Take him there! Get him a car! Find a helicopter! Mr Grant is important.

J   That's very good of you, Senator.
S   Your boy-friend's cookies, Miss Egan, are going to help me win the support of the President. How long are you thinking of staying in Washington?
J   We intend to stay here two weeks.
S   And I intend to be frontrunner in the race for Governor. I'll be ahead of the other candidates. I ran for Governor last time, but this time I'll succeed in becoming Governor. You'll see.
J   I'd like to know more about your political system, Senator Gatewater.
S   Yes. Well. Now, where shall I start?
J   Would you mind explaining the Constitution?
S   Well, in 1787 . . .

	(secretary interrupts again)	S	Mr and Mrs Turpin having tea with Mr Grant?
P	Excuse me –		
S	Stop interrupting, Miss Pendlebury.	P	Yes. The President is going to make a new trade agreement with Great Britain, for importing Mr Grant's cookies –
P	There was a call from the White House, sir.		
S	Why didn't you tell me?		
P	I didn't want to disturb you, sir.	J	So you'll get the President's support –
S	Well, you've begun disturbing me now, Miss Pendlebury. Carry on!	S	Maybe I'll be Trade Secretary or . . .
P	The President called –	J	*(interrupting)* Secretary of State. After all, this will be an important international agreement . . . .
S	Oh, my God! Give me another cookie, Miss Pendlebury.		
P	He said, "Thank you for sending Mr Grant to the White House."		
S	But I didn't send him to the White House.		
P	No, Senator. I sent him. Mr Grant was sightseeing, and he wanted to go to the White House, and you told me –		
S	Well, what happened? Go on! You keep stopping.		
P	You keep stopping me, sir. Mr Grant is having tea with the President and the First Lady –		

The White House, Washington D.C.

40 B Questions

What are the two Houses of Congress called?
What is the American parliament called?
Where is the seat of the American parliament?
What's the official residence of the American President?
How often can the President be re-elected?
When do Presidential elections take place?
Name the two main political parties in the United States.
Who is the chief executive in each state?
How many Senators are there in the US?
For what period of time are Senators elected?
The minister who advises the President on foreign affairs is called...?

40 C And you?

What is the Head of State in the Federal Republic of Germany called?
Compare his office with that of the American President.

40 D The ing-form (II)

a) ing-form after certain verbs

He **enjoys eating** cookies.	*Er ißt gerne Kekse.*
I **don't mind queueing**	*Es macht mir nichts aus, anzustehen.*
We **dislike waiting.**	*Wir warten nicht gerne.*

Nach folgenden hier aufgeführten Verben muß die ing-Form stehen:

admit	detest	finish	mention
appreciate	dislike	forgive	mind
avoid	enjoy	give up	miss
can't help	excuse	imagine	pardon
can't stand	feel like	keep	practise

b) ing-form after verb + preposition

I've been looking forward to giving an interview.	*Ich habe mich darauf gefreut, ein Interview zu geben.*
I apologise for interrupting you, Senator.	*Es tut mir leid, wenn ich Sie unterbreche, Senator.*
How long **are you thinking of staying** in Washington?	*Wie lange beabsichtigen Sie, in Washington zu bleiben?*

Die ing-Form muß immer stehen nach der Verbindung Verb + Präposition. Hierzu gehören folgende Verben:

apologise for	*sich entschuldigen wegen*
believe in	*glauben an, trauen*
care about	*sich kümmern um, sich sorgen um*
complain about	*sich beschweren über*
concentrate on	*sich konzentrieren auf*
dream (about) of	*träumen von*
insist on	*bestehen auf*
look forward to	*sich freuen auf*
object to	*protestieren, einwenden*
prevent from	*abhalten von, hindern an*
rely on	*sich verlassen auf*
specialise in	*sich spezialisieren auf*
succeed in	*gelingen*
talk about (of)	*sprechen über (von)*
thank for	*danken für*
think (about) of	*denken an*
worry about	*sich ärgern über*

Nach "rely on" ist auch Objekt + Infinitiv mit "to" möglich, z. B.: Can I rely on you to come?

c) ing-form after certain expressions

It's no use trying to find your way with such a small map.	*Es hat keinen Sinn, Zweck . . .*
Is it really worth walking around Washington all day?	*Ist es wirklich wert, daß . . .*
It's no good calling him.	*Es ist zwecklos . . .*
	Es hat keinen Sinn . . .
It's a pleasure being here.	*Es ist ein Vergnügen . . .*
He's busy sightseeing.	*Er ist damit beschäftigt . . .*

Nach "it's a pleasure . . ." ist auch der Infinitiv mit "to" möglich: It's a pleasure to be here.

40 E Complete the sentences.
Use the ing-form and where necessary the correct preposition:

I'm sure you'll soon succeed … English fluently. (speak)
Don't prevent him … (learn)
I've given … (smoke)
It's no use … that I enjoyed it. (say)
We thought … across the States. (drive)
People don't mind … in front of the White House. (queue)
Someone suggested … out for lunch. (go)
Would you mind … the window? (close)
It's a pleasure … in Washington. (be)
I don't object … on Sundays. (work)
It's no use … to find excuses. (try)

40 F The ing-form with pronouns or nouns

Excuse me interrupting, Senator.	*Entschuldigen Sie, wenn ich Sie unterbreche, Senator.*
Do you mind me smoking a pipe?	*Macht es Ihnen etwas aus, wenn ich eine Pfeife rauche?*
I can't imagine David forgetting to come.	*Ich kann mir nicht vorstellen, daß David vergessen hat zu kommen.*

Das Sinnsubjekt (= logische Subjekt) dieser ing-Konstruktion kann durch ein vor der ing-Form stehendes Pronomen oder Substantiv ausgedrückt werden. In der gesprochenen Sprache verwendet man die Objektpronomen me, you, him, her, it, us, them. In der Schriftsprache finden Sie meistens die Pronomen my, your, his etc., bzw. bei Substantiven das Genitiv-s. Excuse my interrupting. Do you mind my smoking a pipe? I can't imagine David's forgetting to come.

40 G Complete the sentences. Use the pronouns as in the spoken language:

Example

> Do you mind ... a suggestion? (I, make)
> Do you mind me making a suggestion?

Beispiel

I don't like ... the conference. (she, interrupt)
Please excuse ... you by your first name. (we, call)
She doesn't like ... late every time. (he, come)
You must forgive ... him. (we, interrupt)
Fancy ... with us for six months. (he, live)
I remember ... to come to our party. (they, forget)
We can't understand ... through Central Park alone. (you, walk)

40 H ing-form or to-infinitive   **ing-Form oder Infinitiv mit "to"**

He began talking.	He began to talk.
I prefer working in the evening.	I prefer to work in the evening.
I don't like dancing.	I don't like to dance tonight.

Die ing-Form berührt sich häufig mit dem Infinitiv. Nach einigen Verben wie z. B. begin, continue, hate, intend, like, love, prefer kann sowohl die ing-Form als auch der Infinitiv mit "to" stehen. Dabei beschreibt die ing-Form mehr eine allgemeingültige Aussage, der Infinitiv mit "to" mehr einen bestimmten Einzelfall.
Wichtig: Nach "would like" oder "would love" kann nur der Infinitiv mit "to" stehen: I'd like to know more about America. I'd love to go there next year.

40 I Complete the following sentences with the ing-form or the to-infinitive. Mark the sentences where both structures are possible:

What do you intend ... today? (do)
I'd love ... you. (come and see)
He'd like ... a glass of wine. (drink)
I enjoy ... (travel)
Some people hate ... (queue)
I prefer ... (walk)
She doesn't mind ... disturbed while she's working. (be)

40 J Vocabulary Practice

Find words in dialogue 40 A that mean the following:
to disturb – it's nice – biscuit – to produce

40 K Who was this man? (CB)

He was born in 1917 near Boston, Massachusetts, of Irish-American parents. He went to Harvard University and studied political science. During World War II he was seriously wounded. After the war he worked as a press correspondent and covered the Potsdam Conference. He was only 29 years old when he entered the House of Representatives. In 1953 he became a Senator. Seven years later he was nominated Presidential candidate of the Democratic Party. In November 1960 he won the election and entered the White House as the 35th President. His term of office was short. On November 22, 1963, he was killed by an assassin in Dallas, Texas. He's buried in the Arlington Cemetery on the outskirts of Washington.
Here's a quotation from his inaugural address. "My fellow-citizens of the world, ask not what America will do for you, but what together we can do for the freedom of man."

40 L Find a synonym or definition of the words or expressions underlined:

seriously wounded
He covered a conference.
term of office

assassin
the outskirts of Washington
inaugural address

40 M Situation – Say it in English

Sie sind zu Besuch in Washington. Fragen Sie jemanden, ob er Ihnen den Weg zum Weißen Haus erklären kann.
Fragen Sie, wie lange Sie brauchen, um dorthin zu kommen.
Ihr Gesprächspartner sagt, daß es zu Fuß ein Weg von ungefähr einer halben Stunde ist.
Fragen Sie, ob Sie das Weiße Haus besichtigen können.
Ihr Gesprächspartner sagt, daß vor dem Weißen Haus immer eine lange Schlange steht.
Bedanken Sie sich dafür, daß Ihr Gesprächspartner Sie gewarnt hat.
Sagen Sie, daß es Ihnen nichts ausmacht, anzustehen.

40 N Summary

This time Jane and her boy-friend were visiting Washington D.C. They had difficulty finding their way because their map was so small, and then Jane had to leave Russell to go and interview a Senator, Senator Gatewater, in his office on Capitol Hill. The Senator's secretary, Miss Pendlebury, showed Jane into the Senator's office, where the Senator was eating cookies – an American word for biscuits. Jane said her boy-friend manufactured cookies. Senator Gatewater found this very interesting, as President Turpin was very fond of eating cookies, and since it was election year, the President's support was very important.

He offered Jane some cookies and began to answer her questions about the US Constitution, but he was interrupted by Miss Pendlebury, who said that Russell Grant had called to say he was lost in Washington – he wanted to go to the White House. Senator Gatewater told her to get Russell a car or find him a helicopter – after all, he was important. Then the Senator went on with his explanation until Miss Pendlebury interrupted him again. There'd been a call from the White House! Russell was having tea with the President and Mrs Turpin, and they were discussing a new trade agreement with Great Britain to import Russell's cookies!

Have another cookie

Vocabulary **Wortschatz**

40			
	site	saɪt	Gelände
	is based on	ɪz 'beɪst ɒn	beruht auf
	principle	'prɪnsɪpl	Grundsatz
	to divide	tə dɪ'vaɪd	trennen, aufteilen
	branch	brɑːntʃ	Abteilung, Zweig
	Executive branch	ɪg'zekjʊtɪv brɑːntʃ	Exekutive, vollziehende Gewalt
	to head	tə 'hed	anführen
	Legislative branch	'ledʒɪslətɪv brɑːntʃ	Legislative, gesetzgebende Gewalt
	Congress	'kɒŋgres	Kongreß, Parlament
	Senate	'senət	Senat
	House of Representatives	'haʊs əv reprɪ'zentətɪvz	Repräsentantenhaus
	Judicial branch	dʒuː'dɪʃl brɑːntʃ	Justiz
	Supreme Court	sʊ'priːm 'kɔːt	Oberster Gerichtshof
	to limit	tə 'lɪmɪt	begrenzen, beschränken
	to prevent	tə prɪ'vent	verhindern, abhalten von
	to gain	tə 'geɪn	gewinnen
	White House	'waɪt haʊs	Weißes Haus *(in Washington)* *Sitz des amerikanischen Präsidenten*
	a four-year term of office	ə 'fɔː jɜː 'tɜːm əv 'ɒfɪs	eine vierjährige Amtszeit, -periode

to re-elect	tə ˈriːɪˈlekt	wiederwählen
the Democrats	ðə ˈdeməkræts	die Demokraten, die Demokratische Partei
the Republicans	ðə rɪˈpʌblɪkənz	die Republikaner, die Republikanische Partei
the Capitol	ðə ˈkæpɪtl	das Kapitol *(das Kongreßgebäude in Washington)*
to introduce new laws	tʊ ˈɪntrədjuːs njuː ˈlɔːz	neue Gesetzesvorlagen einbringen
court	kɔːt	Gericht
whether	weðə	ob
to be in line with	tə ˈbɪ ɪn ˈlaɪn wɪð	übereinstimmen mit
Governor	ˈgʌvənə	Gouverneur *(höchster Repräsentant eines amerikanischen Bundesstaates)*
federal	ˈfedrəl	Bundes-

40 A

pedestrian crossing	pəˈdestrɪən ˈkrɒsɪŋ	Fußgänger-Übergang
it's no use	ɪts ˈnəʊ ˈjuːs	es hat keinen Sinn
such	sʌtʃ	solch, derartig, so, solch ein(e)
we don't even know	wɪ ˈdəʊnt iːvn ˈnəʊ	wir wissen nicht einmal
portrait gallery	ˈpɔːtrət gælərɪ	Gemäldegalerie
to get tired	tə get ˈtaɪəd	müde werden
to interview	tʊ ˈɪntəvjuː	interviewen, befragen
Senator	ˈsenətə	Senator
yeah! *(AE fam.)*	jeə	ja
to show s.b. in	tə ʃəʊ ˈɪn	jdn. hereinführen
hill	hɪl	Hügel
as of now	ˈæz əv ˈnaʊ	von jetzt an
interruption	ɪntəˈrʌpʃn	Unterbrechung, Störung
cookie *(AE)*	ˈkʊkɪ	Keks, Plätzchen
biscuit *(BE)*	ˈbɪskɪt	Keks, Plätzchen
all day long	ˈɔːl deɪ ˈlɒŋ	den ganzen Tag
support	səˈpɔːt	Unterstützung, Hilfe
to deny	tə dɪˈnaɪ	(ver)leugnen, bestreiten
defence *(BE)*, defense *(AE)*	dɪˈfens	Verteidigung, Schutz
way of life	ˈweɪ əv ˈlaɪf	Lebensweise, -art
to manufacture	tə mænjʊˈfæktʃə	herstellen, produzieren
gee *(AE)*	dʒiː	du lieber Himmel! du meine Güte!
FBI = Federal Bureau of Investigation	ˈef ˈbiː ˈaɪ = ˈfedrəl ˈbjʊərəʊ əv ɪnvestɪˈgeɪʃn	Bundeskriminalamt *(USA)*
to run for a post *(AE)*	tə ˈrʌn fər ə ˈpəʊst	für einen Posten kandidieren
he's gotten lost *(AE; BE = got)*	hiːz ˈgɒtn ˈlɒst	er hat sich verirrt
helicopter	ˈhelɪkɒptə	Hubschrauber
frontrunner	ˈfrʌntˈrʌnə	Spitzenkandidat(in)

	race	reɪs	Wettlauf, Wettrennen
	to be ahead of	tə bɪ əˈhed əv	voraus sein, vorne liegen
	to succeed in	tə səkˈsiːd ɪn	gelingen
	to disturb	tə dɪˈstɜːb	stören, unterbrechen
	carry on!	ˈkærɪ ˈɒn	fahren Sie fort! machen Sie weiter!
	trade agreement	ˈtreɪd əgriːmənt	Handelsabkommen
	to import	tʊ ɪmˈpɔːt	importieren, einführen
	secretary *(AE; BE = minister)*	ˈsekrətrɪ, ˈmɪnɪstə	Minister(in)
	Trade Secretary *(AE)*	ˈtreɪd sekrətrɪ	Außenhandelsminister(in)
	Secretary of State *(AE)*	ˈsekrətrɪ əv ˈsteɪt	Außenminister(in)
40 B	to take place	tə ˈteɪk ˈpleɪs	stattfinden
	period of time	ˈpɪərɪəd əv ˈtaɪm	Zeitraum
	foreign affairs	ˈfɒrən əˈfeəz	auswärtige Angelegenheiten
40 D	to appreciate	tʊ əˈpriːʃɪeɪt	schätzen
	to avoid	tʊ əˈvɔɪd	vermeiden
	can't help	ˈkɑːnt ˈhelp	nicht helfen können
	can't stand	ˈkɑːnt ˈstænd	nicht ertragen, ausstehen können
	to detest	tə dɪˈtest	hassen, verabscheuen
	to pardon	tə ˈpɑːdn	verzeihen
	to practise *(AE: to practice)*	tə ˈpræktɪs	üben
	to care about	tə ˈkeər əbaʊt	sich kümmern um
	to concentrate on	tə ˈkɒnsəntreɪt ɒn	sich konzentrieren auf
	to object to	tʊ əbˈdʒekt tə	protestieren, einwenden
	to rely on	tə rɪˈlaɪ ɒn	sich verlassen auf
	to worry about	tə ˈwʌrɪ əbaʊt	sich ärgern über
	it's no good	ɪts ˈnəʊ ˈgʊd	es ist zwecklos, es hat keinen Sinn
40 G	suggestion	səˈdʒestʃən	Vorschlag
40 H	to continue	tə kənˈtɪnjuː	fortfahren, weitermachen
40 K	political science	pəˈlɪtɪkl ˈsaɪəns	Politikwissenschaften
	wounded	ˈwuːndɪd	verwundet
	correspondent	kɒrɪˈspɒndənt	Berichterstatter(in)
	to enter	tʊ ˈentə	eintreten, einziehen in
	to nominate	tə ˈnɒmɪneɪt	ernennen, aufstellen
	assassin	əˈsæsɪn	Mörder (eines Politikers)
	buried	ˈberɪd	begraben, beerdigt
	cemetery	ˈsemətrɪ	Friedhof
	outskirts	ˈaʊtskɜːts	Stadtrand, Peripherie
	quotation	kwəʊˈteɪʃn	Zitat
	inaugural address	ɪˈnɔːgjʊrəl əˈdres	Antrittsrede
	fellow-citizen	ˈfeləʊ ˈsɪtɪzn	Mitbürger(in)
40 L	gravely	ˈgreɪvlɪ	ernst(haft), schwer
	to hold office	tə ˈhəʊld ˈɒfɪs	im Amt sein

UNIT 41

Manhattan, New York City

The Big Apple is a nickname for New York City. And Manhattan, the most famous island in the world, is the very heart of the city. It includes everything that most people think of when they say New York: the financial district with Wall Street and the New York Stock Exchange, Fifth Avenue with all its shops and museums, the Empire State Building, Rockefeller Center, the United Nations Building, Broadway as well as Lincoln Center, the home of all the arts: the Metropolitan Opera House, the New York State Theater and the Avery Fisher Hall, known as Philharmonic Hall.

Finding one's way around New York City is very simple. The streets and avenues are numbered.

When they're giving directions, Americans often say "That's three (or four, or five, etc.) blocks away." A block is a group of buildings surrounded on all four sides by streets. It's quite common to give a corner address by giving the point where a street and an avenue meet, for example 96th and Lexington.

41 A Crime in the City

(F = Frenchie, L = Lauren, W = Waitress, A = Attendant, N = Newscaster, Man)

(At a lunch counter in a deli-restaurant in New York City)
F   Oh! So sorry.
L   Excuse me. Is this seat taken?
F   No. Of course it's free – for you.
L   Gee, thanks. Thanks a lot.
    I haven't seen you here before.
F   No, you haven't. It's my first time in New York.
L   Well, you can spend your whole life at this counter waiting to be served. But you gotta hand it to them. They have the best pastrami in town. Say! You're British, aren't you?

F English, actually.
L My name's Schmidt. Lauren Schmidt.
F ffrench. The Honourable Pilkington Booth ffrench. With two f's.
L The Honourable?
  Son of a lord? No kidding? You here on vacation?
F I suppose it's a sort of holiday. I'll do a bit of sightseeing. Maybe a bit of work, too.
L Oh! What sort of work?
F Oh, business – you know –
L Real estate? Stock market? Wall Street?
F Anything to do with money, actually. I'll take what comes along.
L So what do you think of the Big Apple?
F Big Apple?
L New York. We call it the Big Apple.
F Fine city. Romantic . . .
L Romantic? Let me give you a piece of advice. For free! Take care where you go in this city. It's a mighty rough place. There's a lot of crime around.
F What about your police? They can handle it, I'm sure.
L Yes. But they're very busy a lot of the time. Too busy to keep an eye on everybody.
F Oh, I see. A useful piece of information. Thank you.
L So take care where you go. Specially at night. Keep away from Central Park. And mind how you go on the subway.
F Subway? Ah, yes. Not quite like the London Underground. Excuse me. I must be going. But I'd like to see you again.
L Sure! What about here? Around noon, tomorrow.
F Yes. Splendid! Well, cheerio!
L Have a good day! And take care!
  (Frenchie leaves)
W Hey, mister! Your check!
L Don't worry. He'll be back tomorrow. Now, how about a pastrami on rye and a coke?
W All right, lady. You got it.

(Frenchie somewhere in New York City, knocking at a door)

F Good afternoon. Joe sent me. From London.
  (the door is opened from inside)
F Silent type, isn't he?
Man Guess so. You're Frenchie, aren't you?
F At the moment I'm the Honourable Pilkington Booth ffrench, with two . . .
Man Aw, you can cut that out with me. You're Frenchie and you're here for a piece of the action. Right?
F Well, I certainly need a bit of cash.
Man You got it. On my terms. I say what goes round here. OK?

F	OK.
Man	Right. It's a hold-up. A liquor store. Uptown. Corner of 96th and Lexington.
F	All right. Sounds fine.
	(man gives him a gun)
Man	You'll need a piece. Here!
F	Oh, no. I don't like guns.
Man	I said a hold-up.
F	Oh, all right. I'll take it.
Man	You have transportation? You have a car?
F	No. But I've got a map. Now, let's see. I'll take a cab to Grand Central Station. Then Underground – sorry, the subway. Take the subway to Times Square. That's down the stairs and into the line 7. Change to line 1 for West 59th Street. Walk through Lincoln Center and across Central Park. That takes me out on Fifth Avenue. A bus uptown to 96th Street. Walk three blocks and I'm there.
Man	You crazy? That's round the world.
F	I like to make sure I'm not being followed.
Man	Well, you sure will be followed if you wear those clothes . . .
F	Oh, I'll change my jacket and my trousers. And I'll put on this pair of spectacles. And . . .
Man	OK. Do anything you like, but get there just before closing. It's the end of the week, so you should get about five grand. Bring it back here. We'll split it fifty-fifty.
F	Two thousand five hundred dollars each, eh?
Man	Say! He's quite smart after all.
F	I'll be off, then. See you later.
Man	Make sure that you do. It wouldn't be healthy otherwise. Get hold of Larry for me and tell him that if he doesn't . . .

	(scene changes to liquor store)
F	That's good. But don't move for two minutes because you might get hurt if you do.
A	Please, mister. I didn't do anything. I didn't move.
F	No. But I nearly forgot the cash.
A	I didn't move.
F	And I forgot my map. I'd be lost without it.

Lincoln Center, New York City

	(scene changes back to deli-restaurant)
N	. . . and the weather in New York City will be hot again, with a little light rain . . .
W	What can I get you?
F	I'm waiting for someone, actually. But I'll have a cup of coffee.
N	And here is the local news. The police are looking for a man who held up a liquor store last night and took five thousand dollars at gunpoint. The police have issued the following description of the man, who is thought to be a well-known London criminal, Frenchie Boots, alias the Honourable Pilkington Booth. He is about six feet tall, a hundred and eighty pounds, with fair hair . . .

	(F is making for the door when he comes up against Lauren)	L	I'd like to see the contents of that bag, officer.
F	Ah, hello. I'm afraid I've got to leave. I'm in a bit of a hurry.	F	I think there's been some kind of mistake.
L	Lauren Schmidt, lieutenant, 31st Precinct. Sorry, Frenchie. I'm taking you in for armed robbery.	L	It was your mistake, Frenchie. I gave you a piece of advice, remember? Take care where you go at night.

41 B Questions

Who is Lauren?
What sort of crime did Frenchie commit?
What did he hold up?
What do the police know about Frenchie?
How much money did Frenchie take?
What description did the newscaster give of Frenchie?

41 C And you?

What sort of penalty would you suggest for Frenchie?
What do you think are the natural causes of crime?
Make suggestions as to how the police can prevent robbery.

41 D Use of singular and plural — Verwendung von Singular und Plural

a) English singular for German plural

He gave me **some advice**.	*einige Ratschläge*
She has made **some progress**.	*einige Fortschritte*
The furniture was damaged.	*die Möbel*
Your knowledge of English is excellent.	*Ihre Englischkenntnisse*
Thank you for **all the information.**	*für alle Auskünfte*

Dem englischen Singular entspricht hier ein deutscher Plural. Einige dieser Substantive können durch Zusätze wie "a pair of", "a bit of", "a piece of", "some" zählbar gemacht werden: Let me give you a piece of advice, *einen Rat*.

b) English plural for German singular

I'll change **my trousers**.	*meine Hose*
I'll put on **this pair of spectacles**.	*diese Brille*
I'd like to see **the contents** of the bag.	*den Inhalt*
He fell down **the stairs**.	*die Treppe*

Zu den englischen Pluralwörtern, denen ein deutscher Singular entspricht, gehören: contents, glasses, jeans, pants, pliers, scissors, shorts, spectacles, stairs, trousers. Durch den Zusatz von "a pair of" können die Substantive glasses, jeans, pants, pliers, scissors, shorts, spectacles und trousers zählbar gemacht werden.

c) Nouns which occur only in the plural

The police are here.	*Die Polizei ist da.*
The people were investigating the case.	*Die Leute untersuchten den Fall (gingen der Sache nach).*
The district of **the poor**.	*Das Viertel der Armen, das Armenviertel.*

Bei Sammelbegriffen, die als Vielfalt aufgefaßt werden, wie police, people, steht das Verb im Plural. Beachten Sie: the poor, *die Armen*. Aber: the blacks, *die Schwarzen*, mit Plural -s.

d) Nouns which occur only in the singular

Here is **the local news**.	*Hier sind die Lokalnachrichten.*
The United States is a big country.	*Die Vereinigten Staaten sind ein großes Land.*

Pluralwörter wie "news" oder "the United States" werden als Einheit aufgefaßt. Das Verb steht deshalb im Singular.

41 E   Translate:

Das ist eine interessante Information.
Könnten Sie mir bitte eine Schere geben?
Diese Brille ist altmodisch.
Die Vereinigten Staaten haben viele Arbeitslose.
Ich werde Ihnen einen nützlichen Rat geben.
Können Sie die Möbel morgen bringen?
Vielen Dank für die Auskünfte.
Er hat sich gestern bei Bloomingdale drei Jeans gekauft.
Ich möchte den Inhalt Ihrer Brieftasche sehen.
Es sind große Fortschritte gemacht worden auf dem Gebiet (in the field of) der Technik.

41 F   Put in the correct tense – simple past or present perfect:

I ... you here before. (not see)
The police are looking for a man who ... a liquor store last night and ... $5,000. (hold up, take)
The police ... the following description. (issue)
Humphrey ... the Empire State Building. (never climb)
Fast food chains ... Europe now. (reach)
She ... to the Metropolitan Museum last Friday. (go)
In our last programme Jane ... a Senator. (interview)
There ... an excellent performance of "The Magic Flute" yesterday evening in the Metropolitan Opera House. (be)

41 G Vocabulary Practice

What do these words or expressions mean?

counter – terms – to split – to take somebody in – mistake – to issue

41 H Phonetics

Write down the words that are pronounced as follows:

/siːt/   /ˈæktʃʊəlɪ/   /ˈhɒlədɪ/   /ˈwɔːl striːt/   /ə ˈpiːs əv ədˈvaɪs/   /təˈmɒrəʊ/

/teɪk ˈkeə/   /kləʊðz/   /kæʃ/   /kʌp/

41 I What would you say if …

– you wanted to introduce your boy-friend (girl-friend) to some other friends of yours?
– you were in New York and you wanted to know how to get to the Guggenheim Museum?
– you wanted to know the time?
– you wanted to change a dollar bill?
– somebody said to you he was sorry? (Say it in American English.)

41 J Invent an ending to this letter

Dear David,

When I was in New York last week, I went shopping at Bloomingdale's. It was about four o'clock in the afternoon and there were a lot of people in the leather goods department. And guess what happened! I watched a young woman who shoplifted an expensive bag. I was so surprised that I couldn't say anything . . . .

41 K A taste of America

Fast food is now found all over the world. Not only hamburgers, but fried chicken and hot dogs are eaten everywhere. People are in a hurry, they want a quick snack.

In big American cities you can eat the national dishes of every country in the world. Where you eat depends on how much money you want to spend. You can get excellent steaks or seafood in more expensive restaurants. If you don't want to spend too much, you can go to a snack bar, a coffee shop, a deli-restaurant, a sidewalk café, or to one of the fast food chains. A typical dish is a Pastrami – a kind of spiced smoked beef served on black rye bread.

41 L Some American slang expressions from our story

no kidding	*kein Scherz, echt*
gee	*du liebe Güte! du lieber Himmel!*
five grand	*fünftausend Dollar*
you gotta hand it to them	*das muß man ihnen lassen*
you crazy?	*bist du wahnsinnig?*
you got it?	*hast du verstanden?*
cut it out!	*hör auf damit! laß den Quatsch!*

41 M Situation – Say it in English

Fragen Sie höflich, ob dieser Platz frei ist.
Sagen Sie, daß es kaum sicher ist, durch den Central Park zu gehen.
Sie werden nach dem Weg zum Mayflower Hotel gefragt:
Sagen Sie Ihrem Gesprächspartner, daß er die U-Bahn bis Columbus Circle nehmen und dann einen Häuserblock gehen soll, dann kommt er zum Mayflower Hotel.
Raten Sie ihm, vorsichtig zu sein, wenn er in New York U-Bahn fährt.
Raten Sie ihm, sich vor Taschendieben (pickpockets) in acht zu nehmen.
Raten Sie ihm, aufzupassen, wo er hingeht.
Wünschen Sie ihm einen schönen Tag.
Ihr Gesprächspartner bedankt sich vielmals für Ihre Auskünfte und den nützlichen Rat.
Sagen Sie, daß Sie das gern getan haben.

41 N Summary

Two strangers met in a restaurant in New York. One was Lauren Schmidt, a New Yorker. The other said his name was the Honourable Pilkington Booth ffrench. He had an English accent, and Lauren seemed impressed that he was the son of a lord. She gave him an important piece of advice – to take care where he went in New York and to be careful on the subway. They arranged to meet again the following day – and he went out without paying. A man he visited in a very run-down part of the city called him "Frenchie", and gave him details of a hold-up he had planned. He was to hold up a liquor store in uptown New York and share the money with him. Frenchie successfully held up the liquor store. The next day he went back to the delicatessen restaurant for his meeting with Lauren. In the deli, the television news reported the hold-up and gave a description of Frenchie. He was about to leave when he bumped into Lauren. She turned out to be a woman police officer, and arrested him for armed robbery. As she took him away, she reminded him of the piece of advice she'd given him – to take care where he went!

Take care where you go

Vocabulary   **Wortschatz**

41
Big Apple	ˈbɪg ˈæpl	*(fam. für New York)*
nickname	ˈnɪkneɪm	Spitzname
United Nations	jʊˈnaɪtɪd ˈneɪʃnz	Vereinte Nationen
to number	tə ˈnʌmbə	numerieren
direction	dəˈrekʃn	Richtung
block	blɒk	*(AE)* Häuserblock
surrounded	səˈraʊndɪd	umgeben

41 A
waitress	ˈweɪtrəs	Kellnerin, Bedienung
attendant	əˈtendənt	Bedienstete(r), Verkäufer(in)
newscaster	ˈnjuːzkɑːstə	Nachrichtensprecher(in)
counter	ˈkaʊntə	Theke
deli(catessen)	ˈdelɪ, delɪkəˈtesn	Feinkostladen, Feinkostrestaurant
you gotta hand it to them *(slang)*	jə ˈgɒtə ˈhænd ɪt tə ðəm	das muß man ihnen lassen
honourable	ˈhɒnrəbl	ehrenwert(-e, -er)
lord	lɔːd	Lord
no kidding *(slang)*	ˈnəʊ ˈkɪdɪŋ	kein Scherz, echt
vacation	veɪˈkeɪʃn	*(AE)* Ferien
real estate *(AE)*	ˈrɪəl əˈsteɪt	Grundbesitz
stock market	ˈstɒk mɑːkɪt	Wertpapierbörse
romantic	rəˈmæntɪk	romantisch
a piece of advice	ə ˈpiːs əv ədˈvaɪs	ein Rat
for free *(AE)*	fə ˈfriː	umsonst
to take care	tə teɪk ˈkeə	vorsichtig sein
rough	rʌf	ungemütlich, roh, brutal
to handle s.th.	tə hændl	etw. im Griff haben
to keep an eye on s.th. or s.b.	tə ˈkiːp ən ˈaɪ ɒn	etw. oder jdn. im Auge behalten
specially	ˈspeʃlɪ	besonders
to keep away from	tə kiːp əˈweɪ frəm	sich fernhalten von
around noon	əraʊnd ˈnuːn	gegen Mittag
cheerio *(BE)*	ˈtʃɪərɪˈəʊ	mach's gut! alles Gute!
check	tʃek	*(AE)* Rechnung
rye	raɪ	Roggen(brot)
coke	kəʊk	Cola
to knock at a door	tə ˈnɒk ət ə ˈdɔː	an eine Tür klopfen
silent	ˈsaɪlənt	schweigsam
guess so *(AE)*	ˈges ˈsəʊ	vermutlich
cash	kæʃ	Bargeld
on my terms	ɒn ˈmaɪ ˈtɜːms	zu meinen Bedingungen
hold-up	ˈhəʊldʌp	Überfall
liquor store	ˈlɪkə stɔː	Spirituosenladen

	uptown *(AE)*	ˈʌptaʊn	im oberen Stadtteil; in den oberen Stadtteil
	gun	gʌn	Pistole, Revolver, „Kanone"
	transportation *(bes. AE)*	trænspɔːˈteɪʃn	Transportmittel
	cab	kæb	Taxi
	stairs	steəz	Treppe
	line	laɪn	Linie
	across	əˈkrɒs	über, durch
	crazy	ˈkreɪzɪ	verrückt, wahnsinnig
	a pair of spectacles (*or:* glasses)	ə ˈpeər əv ˈspektəklz (ˈglɑːsɪz)	eine Brille
	five grand *(slang)*	faɪv ˈgrænd	fünftausend Dollar
	to split	tə ˈsplɪt	aufteilen
	I'll be off	ˈaɪl bɪ ˈɒf	ich gehe, haue ab
	it wouldn't be healthy otherwise	ɪt ˈwʊdnt bɪ ˈhelθɪ ˈʌðəwaɪz	es wäre sonst nicht zuträglich (gesund)
	to get hold of s.b.	tə get ˈhəʊld əv	jdn. zu fassen kriegen
	to move	tə ˈmuːv	sich bewegen, sich rühren
	local news	ˈləʊkl ˈnjuːz	Lokalnachrichten
	at gunpoint	ət ˈgʌnpɔɪnt	mit ausgestreckter Waffe
	to issue	tʊ ˈɪʃuː	herausgeben
	description	dɪˈskrɪpʃn	Beschreibung
	criminal	ˈkrɪmɪnl	Verbrecher
	alias	ˈeɪlɪəs	sonst … genannt
	fair hair	ˈfeə ˈheə	blondes Haar
	lieutenant	*(AE)* luːˈtenənt, *(BE)* lefˈtenənt	Leutnant
	precinct	ˈpriːsɪŋkt	*(AE)* (Polizei-)Bezirk
	to take s.b. in	tə teɪk ˈɪn	jdn. verhaften
	armed robbery	ɑːmd ˈrɒbərɪ	bewaffneter Raubüberfall
	contents	ˈkɒntents	Inhalt
41 B	to commit a crime	tə kəˈmɪt ə ˈkraɪm	ein Verbrechen begehen
41 C	penalty	ˈpenltɪ	Strafe, Strafmaß
41 D	progress	ˈprəʊgres	Fortschritte
	knowledge	ˈnɒlɪdʒ	Wissen, Kenntnisse
	to fall down	tə fɔːl ˈdaʊn	hinunterfallen
	pants	pænts	*(BE)* Unterhose; *(AE)* Hose
	scissors	ˈsɪzəz	Schere
	to investigate	tʊ ɪnˈvestɪgeɪt	nachforschen, untersuchen
	case	keɪs	Fall
41 E	the unemployed	ðɪ ˈʌnɪmˈplɔɪd	die Arbeitslosen
	in the field of	ɪn ðə ˈfiːld əv	auf dem Gebiet von
41 F	fast food chain	ˈfɑːst ˈfuːd tʃeɪn	Schnellimbiß-Kette
	The Magic Flute	ðə ˈmædʒɪk ˈfluːt	Die Zauberflöte

41 G	conditions	kənˈdɪʃnz	Bedingungen
	error	ˈerə	Irrtum
	to publish	tə ˈpʌblɪʃ	veröffentlichen
41 I	dollar bill	ˈdɒlə ˈbɪl	Dollarnote
41 J	ending	ˈendɪŋ	Ende, Schluß
	leather goods	ˈleðə gʊdz	Lederwaren
	to guess	tə ˈges	raten, schätzen
	to shoplift	tə ˈʃɒplɪft	Ladendiebstahl begehen
41 K	hamburger	ˈhæmbɜːgə	Hamburger
	fried chicken	ˈfraɪd ˈtʃɪkɪn	gebratenes Hähnchen
	snack	snæk	Imbiß
	dish	dɪʃ	Gericht
	to depend on	tə dɪˈpend ɒn	abhängen von
	seafood	ˈsiːfuːd	Meeresfrüchte
	sidewalk café *(AE)*	ˈsaɪdwɔːk kəˈfeɪ	Straßencafé
	spiced	spaɪst	gewürzt
	smoked	sməʊkt	geräuchert
	beef	biːf	Rindfleisch
41 M	pickpocket	ˈpɪkpɒkɪt	Taschendieb
41 N	accent	ˈæksnt	Akzent
	to seem	tə ˈsiːm	scheinen
	to arrange	tʊ əˈreɪndʒ	ausmachen, übereinkommen
	the following day	ðə ˈfɒləʊɪŋ ˈdeɪ	am nächsten Tag
	a run-down part of the city	ə ˈrʌndaʊn ˈpɑːt əv ðə ˈsɪti	ein heruntergekommenes Stadtviertel
	to bump into s.b.	tə bʌmp ˈɪntʊ	jdm. in die Arme laufen, jdn. (zufällig) treffen

UNIT 42

Golden Gate Bridge, San Francisco

San Francisco was founded in 1776 by Spanish settlers. They built the Mission Dolores and called the place Yerba Buena. In 1821 it became Mexican territory. The Mexicans controlled it until 1847, when California became part of the United States. In the same year gold was discovered and in 1849 the real gold rush began. Until the Californian gold rush of 1849 San Francisco was a small village. Almost overnight it became a thriving town. Over 100,000 men rushed to California and San Francisco was transformed into a booming metropolis.

In 1906 a terrible earthquake destroyed the city's central area. San Francisco now has about 750,000 inhabitants, and it's the chief port on the Pacific Coast. It's a multicultural city, and it's the gateway to Asia. The Golden Gate Bridge, Chinatown (the largest Chinese community outside Asia), the area around Fisherman's Wharf and the various hills with their magnificent views over the city are only some of San Francisco's famous attractions. Across Oakland Bay Bridge is Berkeley, where the University of California is situated.

42 A On campus

(P = Passenger, J = Jane, R = Russell, C = Carol, Ch = Chuck)

(In San Franciscan Subway – BART)

P   Students?
J   What?
R   Yes. Yes, we are.
P   Bob. Bob Kapolski. Glad to know you.
R   How d'you do? I'm Russell Grant.
J   And I'm Jane Grant.
P   Jane. Married, huh?
J   Excuse me. *(to Russell)* He wants to know if we're married.
R   Well, why don't you tell him?
J   No. No, we're not. We're brother and sister.

P	Oh! And which school are you going to?
J	Now he wants to know which school we're going to.
R	Tell him we're not going to school. We're going to university.
P	Pardon me?
J	Just a minute. You tell him.
R	OK. We're not going to school. We're going to university. University of Berkeley, California.
P	University of Berkeley, eh? A good school. Do you know people in Berkeley?
R	No. Why?
P	Well, I've heard it's difficult to find a place to live there.
R	Bob says that it's difficult to find a place to live in Berkeley.
J	Not for us. We're living on campus. Russell's living in a Fraternity House and I'm in a Sorority House.

(Sorority House, C on the phone)

C	I don't know, Chuck. I really can't think of anybody. Hey, just a minute. Jane has a brother and . . . Jane? My room-mate. The British girl. I told you about her. She's been here for one whole week already. No? Anyway, she has this brother and maybe he can help out. I'll ask her. See ya, Chuck. Chuck! Chuck! Aw! He hung up.
J	What's going on?
C	That was Chuck.
J	Yes. So I gathered.
C	He has a problem.
J	Oh?
C	Well, you know he just loves sports: football, basketball, baseball – you name it.
J	Yes. You told me.
C	Well, he has a game this weekend and he says one of his team can't play. He wants to know if I know anybody who could play and I thought . . .
J	Yes?
C	What about Russell?
J	Russell! Well, I know he likes sport and so on but . . .
C	Chuck would like to know if Russell can play in the ball-game this Saturday.
J	I'm sure he can but . . .
C	And he needs to know if Russell can run fast.
J	Why, yes. But he really doesn't know much about American sport.
C	He can learn.
J	OK. I'll call him.
C	Great! Oh, and another thing . . .
J	What?
C	Chuck wants us to meet him tomorrow morning.

Mission Dolores, San Francisco

(Fast Food Cafeteria)

Ch	Russell, I can't tell you how pleased I am to meet you.
R	Glad to meet you.
Ch	And I want you to know that I am truly grateful, Russ.
R	Pleasure.
Ch	Carol here tells me that you haven't been to a ball-game before, Russ.
R	That's right. I've got four days to learn.

R	Four days!
J	Look, why don't we sit down?
C	Right. Burgers and shakes, you guys? I'm buying.
R	Fine by me.
Ch	And relish.
C	And relish. Come on, Jane. *(J and C off)*
R	Jane tells me that you and Carol have known each other a long time.
Ch	That's right. We met in high school as a matter of fact. I was a senior and she was a junior.
R	A senior what?
Ch	Oh. Um. I was in 12th grade – the last year – and she was in 11th grade.
R	You're not in the same year here, then?
Ch	No, no. I'm a sophomore and she's a freshman. Like you guys.
R	Right. Just beginners. What are you studying, by the way?
Ch	Well, as a matter of fact, Russell, I haven't decided yet. But I think it'll be business administration. It has a future, you know what I mean?
R	Yes, I do. Good idea. *(C and J return each holding a tray containing burgers and shakes and relish)*
C	There you go, guys. With relish. Eat that, Russell. Then you can start training for the ball-game.
J	And I can train to be a cheerleader.

	(players' entrance to baseball park)
Ch	Where are they? Where are Jane and Russell? They're late already.
J	Hi, guys.
R	Huh.
J	U. O. E. D. Will we win? Just wait and see! What do you think?
C	Great! Er – just great! *(Russell comes dressed in American football gear)*
Ch	Russell! But . . . . Jane! For God's sakes. Jane, ask him why he's dressed like that.
J	Why are you dressed like that?
R	*(miming blocking)* Huh. Ugh. Huh.
J	He says it's for the ball-game. Football. American football.
Ch	Football! Oh, no! Tell him, Jane.
J	Tell him what?
Ch	*(pointing at sign)* Tell him – it's a different ball-game.
J	Baseball.

42 B Questions

Who were the first settlers in San Francisco?
What name did they give to the place?
Why did so many people come to San Francisco more than a century ago?
What happened in San Francisco in 1906?
In which university town are Jane and Russell living?
Which ball-game is Russell asked to play?

San Francisco

42 C And you?

What is your opinion about examinations? Are they fair?
Can you describe the educational system in your country?
What sort of adult education is there in your country?

42 D Reported speech (I) — Indirekte Rede

Das Verb der indirekten Rede richtet sich nach der Zeitform des einführenden Satzes.

direkte Rede	indirekte Rede
It's difficult to find a place to live in Berkeley.	Bob says (that) it's difficult to find a place to live in Berkeley.
One of my team can't play.	He says one of his team can't play.
We've known each other a long time.	He tells me they've known each other a long time.

Steht das einführende Verb in der Gegenwart, wird die Zeitform der direkten Rede beibehalten. Aussagen werden in der indirekten Rede häufig mit den Verben "say" und "tell" eingeleitet. Im Englischen steht abweichend vom Deutschen in der indirekten Rede immer der Indikativ, die Wirklichkeitsform: Bob says (that) it's difficult. *Bob sagt, daß es schwierig sei.*

42 E Put the sentences into reported speech:

I'm going to Los Angeles tomorrow. (Bob says …)
We're living on campus. (They say …)
I'm not very well today. (Tell him she …)
We're not Americans. (Jane and Russell say …)
I've lost my map. (Tell her she …)
We're coming to tea on Sunday. (Tell her they …)
I'm studying business administration. (Chuck says …)
I've heard the news. (He says …)

42 F Reported questions (I) — Der Fragesatz in der indirekten Rede

direkte Rede	indirekte Rede
Are you married?	He wants to know if we're married.
Which school do you go to?	He asks which school we go to.

Der Fragesatz in der indirekten Rede kann mit "ask" oder "want to know" eingeleitet werden. Beachten Sie: Der indirekte Fragesatz hat die Wortstellung (Subjekt – Verb – Objekt) des Aussagesatzes.

42 G Change the sentences into reported questions:

Are you tired? (He wants to know …)
How old are you? (He asks …)
Can you run fast? (He asks …)
Have you got a car? (He wants to know …)
Where do you live? (He wants to know …)
Why are you dressed like that? (He asks …)
Which university do you go to? (He asks …)
Do you earn a good salary? (He wants to know …)
Do you like travelling? (He wants to know …)
Who is this man? (He asks …)

42 H Complete the sentences with the correct tense:

Jane and Russell … in the States four weeks ago. (arrive)
Carol and Chuck … each other a long time. (know)
He … yet what to study. (not decide)
Last week Frenchie … for armed robbery. (arrest)
They … on campus for a week. (live)
In 1963 John F. Kennedy … by an assassin. (kill)
Chuck … in 12th grade last year. (be)
Russell … to San Francisco before. (not be)
Senator Gatewater … in Congress for twelve years. (be)

42 I Find the noun from the following words:

know – difficult – live – decide – married – meet – different – important – defend – elect

Make a sentence with each of these nouns.

42 J Education and Sport

In America elementary education begins at the age of six. The first year is known as "first grade" and each year American children go up a grade until they leave school at the age of eighteen from the twelfth grade. So a 6th-grader, for example, is eleven or twelve years old. Elementary school is from 1st to 6th grade, junior high school covers 7th, 8th and sometimes 9th grade and high school goes from 9th or 10th to 12th grade.
After leaving high school, Americans can enter college or university.
A first year student is called a "freshman", a second year student is a "sophomore", a third year student is a "junior" and one who is in his fourth year is a "senior". The students usually take four years to complete a bachelor's degree.
College sport is extremely important in the USA. The main sports are American football (which is a little bit like rugby), baseball, basketball, ice-hockey, and soccer – that's the word the Americans use for European football.

42 K Which definition or synonym goes with each word?

campus	person sharing a room
grade	crowd stimulator
room-mate	college or university grounds
freshman	academic title
degree	first year student
cheerleader	class

42 L Differences in vocabulary

BE	AE	
luggage	baggage	*Gepäck*
pavement	sidewalk	*Gehsteig*
biscuit	cookie	*Keks*
postman	mailman	*Briefträger*
holiday	vacation	*Urlaub, Ferien*
tram	streetcar	*Straßenbahn*
bill	check	*Rechnung*
note	bill	*Note (Geld)*
chemist's	drugstore	*Drogerie*
petrol	gas(oline)	*Benzin*
sweets	candy, candies	*Süßigkeiten*

42 M Some American Writers

JACK LONDON   (1876–1916) He was born in San Francisco and raised on the waterfront. He went to work at a very early age, and participated in the Klondike gold rush. *The Call of the Wild* was a best-seller. His novels and short stories are still popular.

MARK TWAIN   (1835–1910) Before becoming a writer he spent several years as a ship's pilot on the Mississippi. He was a great humorist. Among his bestknown books are *The Adventures of Huckleberry Finn, Tom Sawyer* and *Life on the Mississippi*.

O. HENRY   (1862–1910) was the pen name of William Sidney Porter. He is one of the most widely published of modern authors. He wrote more than 600 short stories with good-humoured comment chiefly on the fortunes of men and women in New York City.

ERNEST HEMINGWAY   (1898–1961) Simple words and short sentences are characteristic of his style. His experiences as a reporter in the Spanish Civil War formed the background of his novel *For Whom the Bell Tolls*. His short novel *The Old Man and the Sea* reflects his favourite subject – man's struggle against a hostile environment. In 1954 he was awarded the Nobel Prize for literature.

42 N Situation – Say it in English

Fragen Sie Ihren Gesprächspartner, auf welche Schule er geht.
Ihr Gesprächspartner hat die Frage nicht verstanden. Wie reagiert er?
Sagen Sie, daß Sie wissen möchten, was er studiert.
Er sagt, daß er Betriebswirtschaft studiert. *(indirekte Rede)*
Sagen Sie, daß Sie gerne wissen möchten, wo er lebt.
Sagen Sie, daß Sie wissen möchten, ob er Sport mag.
Bedanken Sie sich für das Interview.
Wie reagiert Ihr Gesprächspartner (auf amerikanisch)?

42 O Summary ◯◯

Jane and Russell had a conversation with another passenger on BART – the San Francisco Bay Area Rapid Transit, one of the world's most modern city transport systems.

They explained to him that they were brother and sister, and were on their way to Berkeley University, where they were students. They live on the university campus, Jane in a Sorority House and Russell in a Fraternity House.

Carol, Jane's room-mate, was talking to her boy-friend Chuck on the phone when Jane came into the room. Chuck had a problem: he needed another member to play for his team in a baseball game the following weekend. Carol asked Jane if Russell would like to play.

The four met the following day at a cafeteria where they chatted over hamburgers and shakes. Russell agreed to play in the ball-game and promised to practise all the moves, and Jane said she would try to practise as a cheerleader. The day of the game arrived. Chuck and Carol were waiting for Jane and Russell in front of the entrance to the ball park. Russell arrived dressed in full football dress – he had been practising the wrong game!

Use your head to save your feet

Vocabulary / Wortschatz

42

English	Pronunciation	German
Mexican	ˈmeksɪkən	mexikanisch; Mexikaner(in)
California	kælɪˈfɔːnɪə	Kalifornien
gold rush	ˈgəʊld rʌʃ	Goldrausch
overnight	əʊvəˈnaɪt	über Nacht
thriving	ˈθraɪvɪŋ	blühend
to rush	tə ˈrʌʃ	rasen, drängen, stürzen
to transform	tə trɑːnsˈfɔːm	verwandeln, umwandeln
boom	buːm	(Hoch-)Konjunktur, wirtschaftlicher Aufschwung
metropolis	mɪˈtrɒpəlɪs	Metropole, Hauptstadt
earthquake	ˈɜːθkweɪk	Erdbeben
to destroy	tə dɪˈstrɔɪ	zerstören
central area	ˈsentrəl ˈeərɪə	Innenstadt
inhabitant	ɪnˈhæbɪtənt	Einwohner(in)
Pacific coast	pəˈsɪfɪk ˈkəʊst	Pazifikküste
multicultural	ˌmʌltɪˈkʌltʃərəl	von kultureller Vielfalt
gateway	ˈgeɪtweɪ	Tor
Asia	ˈeɪʃə	Asien
Chinese	tʃaɪˈniːz	chinesisch; Chinese, Chinesin
wharf, pl wharves	wɔːf, wɔːvz	Kai, Pier, Hafendamm
various	ˈveərɪəs	verschieden(artig)
magnificent	mægˈnɪfɪsnt	großartig, prächtig
attraction	əˈtrækʃn	Anziehungspunkt, Attraktion

42 A

on campus	ɒn ˈkæmpəs	auf dem Universitätsgelände
pardon me	ˈpɑːdn ˈmiː	wie bitte? Verzeihung!
fraternity	frəˈtɜːnətɪ	(AE) Studentenverbindung
sorority (AE)	səˈrɔːrətɪ	Studentinnenverbindung
room-mate	ˈruːm meɪt	Zimmergenossin, -kameradin, Zimmergenosse, -kamerad
to help out	tə help ˈaʊt	aushelfen, einspringen
to hang up	tə hæŋ ˈʌp	(Telefonhörer) auflegen, einhängen
to gather	tə ˈgæðə	entnehmen, den Schluß ziehen
basketball	ˈbɑːskɪtbɔːl	Basketball
baseball	ˈbeɪsbɔːl	Baseball
he likes sports	hi ˈlaɪks ˈspɔːts	er treibt gerne Sport
cafeteria	kæfəˈtɪərɪə	Selbstbedienungsrestaurant
shake	ʃeɪk	Shake, Mixgetränk
relish	ˈrelɪʃ	Würze
high school (AE)	ˈhaɪ skuːl	höhere Schule
as a matter of fact	əz ə mætər əv ˈfækt	in Wirklichkeit, tatsächlich, eigentlich
senior	ˈsiːnjə	Schüler(in) der 12. Klasse
junior	ˈdʒuːnjə	Schüler(in) der 11. Klasse
grade	greɪd	(AE) Klasse

	sophomore *(AE)*	ˈsɒfəmɔː	Student(in) im 2. Studienjahr
	freshman	ˈfreʃmən	Student(in) im 1. Studienjahr
	business administration	ˈbɪznɪs ədmɪnɪstreɪʃn	Betriebswirtschaft
	tray	treɪ	Tablett
	to train	tə ˈtreɪn	trainieren
	cheerleader *(AE)*	ˈtʃɪəliːdə	Leiter(in) des organisierten Beifalls bei Sportwettkämpfen
	gear	gɪə	*hier:* Ausrüstung
	for God's sake(s)	fə ˈgɒdz ˈseɪk(s)	um Gottes willen
	to mime	tə ˈmaɪm	nachahmen, nachmachen
	to block	tə ˈblɒk	(Ball) abfangen
42 C	educational system	edjʊˈkeɪʃnəl sɪstəm	Erziehungssystem, Bildungssystem
	adult education	əˈdʌlt edjʊkeɪʃn	Erwachsenenbildung
42 I	marriage	ˈmærɪdʒ	Heirat, Hochzeit
42 J	elementary school	elɪˈmentərɪ skuːl	Elementar-, Grundschule
	college	ˈkɒlɪdʒ	College
	to complete	tə kəmˈpliːt	vervollständigen
	bachelor's degree	ˈbætʃələz dɪgriː	unterster akademischer Grad, Staatsexamen
	ice-hockey	ˈaɪs hɒkɪ	Eishockey
42 K	stimulator	ˈstɪmjʊleɪtə	Stimulator, Anreger
	grounds	graʊndz	Grundstück, Gelände
	academic	ækəˈdemɪk	akademisch, wissenschaftlich
42 L	baggage *(AE)*	ˈbægɪdʒ	Gepäck
	pavement *(BE)*	ˈpeɪvmənt	Gehsteig
	sidewalk *(AE)*	ˈsaɪdwɔːk	Gehsteig
	tram *(BE)*	træm	Straßenbahn
	streetcar *(AE)*	ˈstriːtkɑː	Straßenbahn
	chemist's *(BE)*	ˈkemɪsts	Drogerie
	drugstore *(AE)*	ˈdrʌgstɔː	Drogerie
	gas(oline) *(AE)*	gæs, ˈgæsəliːn	Benzin
	sweets *(BE)*	swiːts	Süßigkeiten
	candy, candies *(AE)*	ˈkændɪ, ˈkændɪz	Süßigkeiten
42 M	to raise	tə ˈreɪz	aufziehen, großziehen
	waterfront	ˈwɔːtəfrʌnt	Hafenviertel
	to participate	tə pɑːˈtɪsɪpeɪt	teilnehmen
	best-seller	ˈbestˈselə	Bestseller, Renner
	novel	ˈnɒvl	Roman
	short story	ˈʃɔːt ˈstɔːrɪ	Kurzgeschichte
	ship	ʃɪp	Schiff
	pilot	ˈpaɪlət	Pilot, Lotse
	humorist	ˈhjuːmərɪst	Humorist
	adventure	ədˈventʃə	Abenteuer
	pen name	ˈpen neɪm	Schriftstellername, Pseudonym

good-humoured	ˈgʊd ˈhjuːməd	gut gelaunt; gutmütig
fortune	ˈfɔːtʃən	Schicksal; Glück
sentence	ˈsentəns	Satz
characteristic	kærəktəˈrɪstɪk	charakteristisch, typisch
style	staɪl	Stil
civil war	sɪvl ˈwɔː	Bürgerkrieg
For Whom the Bell Tolls	fə ˈhuːm ðə ˈbel ˈtəʊlz	Wem die Stunde schlägt
to reflect	tə rɪˈflekt	widerspiegeln
struggle	ˈstrʌgl	Kampf
hostile	ˈhɒstaɪl	feindlich
environment	ɪnˈvaɪərənmənt	Umwelt, Umgebung
to award	tʊ əˈwɔːd	*(Preis)* verleihen

42 O Use your head to save your feet — juːz jɔː ˈhed tə seɪv jɔː ˈfiːt — Was man nicht im Kopf hat, muß man in den Beinen haben

UNIT 43

London's theatre world is mainly in the West End. There are about forty theatres showing all sorts of productions, from serious plays to musicals and comedies. Some of the plays shown there go on for a very long time, like *The Mousetrap* by Agatha Christie, which has become something of a national institution. One of England's leading companies is the Royal Shakespeare Company.

The Royal Opera House, Covent Garden, is the home of opera and ballet.

Concerts are given at the Royal Festival Hall, the Queen Elizabeth Hall and the Purcell Room on the South Bank, at the Royal Albert Hall and at the new concert hall in the Barbican Centre. Something which can't be found elsewhere are the Proms, the Promenade Concerts, at which a large part of the audience stands to listen to the music.

43 A Rehearsal

(M = Mary, J = Jane, R = Russell, F = Frank, B = Benson)

WYFORD AMATEUR DRAMATIC SOCIETY presents "DEADLY ERNEST" A modern melodrama by John Benson	
M Hello, Jane. Hello, Russell.	
J Hello, Mary. It's cold, isn't it?	

M *(removing her crash helmet)*
    What was that?
J   I said it was cold.
M   Yes. Very cold.
    What's the play like? Is it any good?
R   No, it's dreadful. Have you read it?
M   *(pulling pullover over her head)*

M	Sorry? I didn't hear what you said.
R	I asked if you'd read the play.
M	No, I haven't. Is Frank directing it?
J	Yes. He'll be here in a moment. He left a message. It says you've got two parts in the play.
M	Oh, wonderful!
R	It's a bad play, I'm afraid. And there are not very good parts.
M	Oh, no! Frank promised he would give me a good part. He told me that my performance in the last play was brilliant.
J	He said my performance was terrible. But he's given me the best part this time.
R	I've got a good part, too. I'm playing Ernest, the villain.
J	He dies in the Last Act. In melodramas the villain always dies in the end. Always.
M	What was that?
J	I said that the villain always dies in the end.
R	Yes. But I kill Mary first. You die in the Second Act.

(Frank, the director, enters)

F	Hello, everybody.
Others	Hello, Frank.
F	Did you see my message?
J	Yes.
F	But you haven't started rehearsing. I told you not to wait. I asked you to start without me. Look! It says clearly: "Don't wait. Start without me."
R	It says a lot of other things, too.
M	And I've just arrived. I was late.

(telephone rings)

J	All right. I'll answer it.
F	Listen! This rehearsal's very important. The writer of the play is coming here – John Benson. He's written lots of plays. He's famous.
R	Your message didn't mention that. It didn't say he was coming.
F	Well, he is coming. And I want first class performances from all of you.

(Jane on the phone)

J	. . . You've broken your arm? You were playing football? Of course you can't come. Oh, yes, I'll tell Frank. Goodbye.

(Jane calls to Frank)

J	Frank!
F	Yes? Who was that?
J	It was Tom. He said he couldn't come to rehearsal.
F	Oh! Why not?
J	He told me that he'd broken his arm. He said he'd been playing football, and . . .
F	But I need him! He's playing the Ghost!
R	Ah! I get killed by the Ghost. In the Last Act.
M	Perhaps you won't be killed now.
F	Of course you'll be killed. In melodrama the villain always dies. Always. Anyway, let's start rehearsing. Come on, everybody.

(some time later)

F	That was fine. You were very good, Mary. I'd like just a little more feeling in your lines. And you, Russell.

F	You can do better. You must be more evil. You're the villain, remember. Right. Let us continue. Act 3, Scene 1.
J	"Love conquers all." That's a silly line.
R	But it's true. Love does conquer all. In melodramas, anyway.
F	What was that?
R	I said that love conquers all.
J	You didn't say it. I said it.
F	Stop arguing!
R	We both said it.
F	I told you to stop arguing. It's not your line, Russell. Now, come on!
J	"Love conquers all. I love you, Ernest. I forgive you."
R	"So you won't tell your father that I killed Elizabeth."
J	"Too late, Ernest. Last night I told him you'd killed her."
R	"Your father's coming now. I can hear him."

(John Benson arrives)

J	You're not my father.
B	No, dear, I'm not.
J	Then who are you?
F	I told you. It's John Benson. I said that he was coming to watch the rehearsal.
J	Well, I didn't hear you. I was answering the telephone.
F	Well, I told the others. And I said he'd written lots of plays, and . . .
B	This isn't one of my best, I'm afraid.
F	The critics liked it. They said it was a great work of art.
J	Well, I'm afraid we're not great artists, Mr Benson.
R	And we haven't got anyone to play the Ghost.
B	I'll play the Ghost. For the rehearsal, anyway.
F	Oh, we are honoured, Mr Benson. Mr Benson said he'd play the Ghost. *(to everyone)* Mr Benson said he would play the Ghost. So we'll rehearse his scene immediately. And I want good performances from everyone. Act 3, Scene 5.
M	That means I'm dead.
B	What was that, dear?
M	I said that I was dead. I died in Act 2.
B	You can play the music for us. The music for the Ghost.
M	All right.
F	The music's there on the record-player, Mary. There are some wonderful lines in this scene, Mr Benson. Immortal lines.
R	"To be or not to be. That is the question." Immortal lines.
F	Those lines are not in this play.
R	I didn't say they were in this play. I just said that they are immortal.
J	From Shakespeare's "Hamlet". And there's a ghost in that play, too.
F	Come on! Let's rehearse.
B	I'm waiting for the music, dear. What's happened to it?
F	I don't know. Mr Benson asked what had happened to the music, Mary!
R	That's not music.
M	But it goes with the Ghost. Sorry! I'll try again.
R	Good Lord!
F	That line's not in the play, Russell.
R	Er – sorry. I thought it was a ghost.
F	Don't be ridiculous.
R	"Stop! Stop, or I'll shoot you."
F	Mary! That's not the right music! *(to Benson)* I'm so sorry.
B	It's all right. I like it.
F	What?
B	I said I liked it.
F	But it doesn't go with the scene.
B	Then I'll change the scene. I'll rewrite it. With a happy ending. A musical ending!

R	Then I won't die.	J	And you said the villain always dies in melodramas.
B	No, of course not.		
F	But it's a melodrama.	B	Not this time, my dear.

43 B Questions

Why is the rehearsal so important?
Why can't Tom come to rehearsal?
What character should he be playing?
Who's John Benson?
What did the critics say about the play?
Why does the author want to change the ending of the play?

43 C And you?

What do you find more interesting – cinema or theatre? Give reasons.
Have you been to a concert lately?
Have you seen a play lately? Which one?

43 D Reported speech (II)   Indirekte Rede

	direkte Rede	indirekte Rede
pres. simple	It's cold.	She said (that) it was cold.
pres. continuous	We're rehearsing.	She said (that) they were rehearsing.
past simple	I left a message.	She said (that) he had left a message.
past continuous	I was playing the villain.	She said (that) he had been playing the villain.
pres. perfect	He has given me the best part.	She said (that) he had given her the best part.
past perfect	I had left a message.	She said he had left a message.
past perfect continuous	I had been playing the villain.	She said he had been playing the villain.
future simple	I'll be back in a moment.	He said he would be back in a moment.
future continuous	I'll be playing the Ghost.	He said he would be playing the Ghost.

Steht das berichtende Verb in der Vergangenheitsform (said, told me usw.), wird die vom Originalsprecher in der direkten Rede verwendete Zeitform im Englischen in der indirekten Rede um eine Zeitstufe zurückgesetzt. Das heißt, die einfache Gegenwart wird zur einfachen Vergangenheit, die Verlaufsform der Gegenwart zur Verlaufsform der Vergangenheit. Einfache und zusammengesetzte Vergangenheit werden beide zur Vorvergangenheit. Die Zeitformen der Vorvergangenheit bleiben in der indirekten Rede unverändert, da hier eine zeitliche Zurücksetzung nicht möglich ist. "Will" wird zu "would", "can" zu "could", "may" zu "might", "must" bzw. "have to" zu "had to".

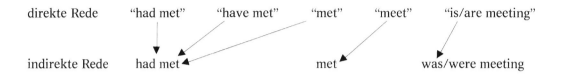

Die Konjunktion "that" ist in der Umgangssprache entbehrlich. Man findet sie eher in der Schriftsprache.

Bei der Umwandlung der direkten Rede in die indirekte Rede wird

here	zu	there	tomorrow	zu	the next day
this	zu	that	yesterday	zu	the day before
these	zu	those	last week	zu	the week before
now	zu	then	a week ago	zu	a week before
today	zu	that day	next week	zu	the following week
			next year	zu	the following year

Ausnahmen vom System der Zeitenfolge: Bei Aussagen von allgemeiner, zeitloser Gültigkeit stehen indirekte Rede und Frage häufig ohne Zeitverschiebung.

> He said (that) the earth is round.
> He said (that) Shakespeare's lines are immortal.

43 E Reported imperative — Befehle oder Aufforderungen in der indirekten Rede

direkte Rede	**indirekte Rede**
Pay attention.	He told her to pay attention.
Answer the telephone, please.	He asked her to answer the telephone.

Befehle oder Aufforderungen werden durch die entsprechende Form von "tell" oder "ask" und den Infinitiv mit "to" ausgedrückt. Die Person, an die der Befehl oder die Aufforderung gerichtet ist, wird durch das Objektpronomen ausgedrückt.

43 F Put the sentences into reported speech:

I am tired. (He said …)
The author is here today. (He said …)
It was cold yesterday. (She said …)
I want more feeling in your lines. (He said …)
Close the window, please. (He asked me …)
I didn't like him. (She said …)
The message was handed to me yesterday. (She said …)
I can't help you. (She said … help me.)
I may need some more actors next year. (He said …)
I won't come tomorrow. (He said …)

43

43 G Reported questions (II)   Der Fragesatz in der indirekten Rede

direkte Rede	**indirekte Rede**
Did you see my message?	He asked her whether (if) she had seen his message.
When will you leave?	She wanted to know when I would leave.

Indirekte Fragesätze werden eingeleitet mit: "He (she) asked, wanted to know, enquired, had no idea" usw.
Bei Entscheidungsfragen steht in der indirekten Frage "if" oder "whether". Fragewörter werden auch in der indirekten Frage beibehalten: She wanted to know **when** I would leave.
Die Zeitverschiebungen entsprechen denen der indirekten Rede.

43 H Put the questions into reported questions:

What's the play like? (He asked)
What happened to the music? (He wanted to know)
Is Frank directing the play? (She asked)
Were you playing football? (She wanted to know)
Who was on the phone? (He asked)
Don't you have a dictionary? (She asked)
Have you spoken to Mr Benson? (He wanted to know)
When will you come back? (She enquired)
How did you get on with the rehearsal? (She asked)
Why can't he cover the story? (He had no idea)

43 I Find other words for the expressions underlined:

The play is <u>dreadful</u>. He left a <u>message</u>.
She <u>wasn't on time</u>. <u>Of course</u> you can't come.
We'll rehearse <u>immediately</u>. You haven't <u>started</u> rehearsing.
Don't be <u>ridiculous</u>. I want <u>first class</u> performances.

43 J Choose the word that best completes each sentence:

They were not interested in … part in the conference.
  a) being   b) taking   c) having   d) doing

After long … the new trade agreement was finally signed.
  a) measurements   b) information   c) negotiations   d) progress

Those … are not in this play.
  a) music   b) sentence   c) directing   d) lines

I want first class … from everyone.
  a) records   b) performances   c) plays   d) advantages

Lauren gave Frenchie a useful piece of …
  a) cash   b) action   c) advice   d) furniture

43 K William Shakespeare (1564–1616)

Shakespeare was the world's greatest dramatist. He was born, it is generally believed, in 1564 in Stratford-upon-Avon. He grew up there and attended the local Grammar School. When he was 18, he married Anne Hathaway who was eight years older than he was. At the age of 22 he left his family and went to London. He became a well-known actor and dramatist as well as a poet. In about 1612 Shakespeare bought a house in Stratford where he lived until his death in 1616. The plays he wrote are still very popular today. Here are some of his most famous tragedies: *Hamlet, Julius Caesar, Romeo and Juliet, Macbeth, Othello, King Lear*. He also wrote historical plays, such as *Henry IV* and *Richard III*, and comedies, such as *The Merry Wives of Windsor, A Midsummer Night's Dream*, and *All's well that ends well*.

43 L Situation – Say it in English

Berichten Sie in der indirekten Rede über ein Gespräch, das Sie mit einer Schauspielerin hatten. Beginnen Sie Ihre Sätze mit: She said …

…, daß sie in Manchester geboren wurde.
…, daß sie in London aufgezogen wurde. (to be brought up)
…, daß sie dort drei Jahre an einer Schauspielschule (drama school) studierte.
…, daß sie gerne in einer Shakespeare-Aufführung mitspielen würde.

Geben Sie ein Telefongespräch mit Tom wieder. Sagen Sie,

…, daß er den Arm gebrochen habe.
…, daß er Cricket gespielt habe.
…, daß er nicht zur Probe kommen könne.

43 M Summary 🎧

Wyford Amateur Dramatic Society was putting on a play, "Deadly Ernest", a modern melodrama by John Benson. One by one, the members of the society arrived in the village hall for a rehearsal. Mary arrived on her motorbike with her crash helmet on, so she didn't hear Jane when she said it was a cold day, and she didn't catch Russell's question when he asked if she had read the play. Russell said he was playing the villain, Ernest, who of course dies at the end of the play, as in all melodramas. Eventually Frank, the director of the play, arrived and said it was important to give a good performance, because the author of the play was coming to watch. Before they could start, however, Tom, one of the actors, phoned to say he couldn't come, as he'd broken his arm while he was playing football. Then they started the rehearsal. In the middle, John Benson arrived. The actors had a problem – they hadn't got anyone to play the Ghost. John Benson said he'd play the Ghost and they carried on rehearsing. But Mary put the wrong music on the record-player – cheerful music instead of melodramatic music. Frank was horrified, but John Benson said he liked it, and said he'd rewrite the play – with a happy ending!

43

*Criticism is easy
and art is difficult*

Vocabulary   **Wortschatz**

43	production	prəˈdʌkʃn	Produktion, Aufführung
	comedy	ˈkɒmədɪ	Komödie
	The Mousetrap	ðə ˈmaʊstræp	Die Mausefalle
	institution	ɪnstɪˈtjuːʃn	Institution, Einrichtung
	to lead	tə ˈliːd	führen, leiten
	ballet	ˈbæleɪ	Ballett
43 A	rehearsal	rɪˈhɜːsl	Theaterprobe
	dramatic	drəˈmætɪk	dramatisch
	society	səˈsaɪətɪ	Gesellschaft
	to present	tə prɪˈzent	aufführen, spielen, darbieten
	deadly	ˈdedlɪ	tödlich
	melodrama	ˈmelədrɑːmə	Melodrama
	to remove	tə rɪˈmuːv	*hier:* ausziehen
	crash helmet	ˈkræʃ helmɪt	Sturzhelm

45

	dreadful	'dredfʊl	furchtbar, schrecklich, entsetzlich
	to direct	tə dəˈrekt	Regie führen
	message	ˈmesɪdʒ	Nachricht, Mitteilung
	brilliant	ˈbrɪljənt	aufsehenerregend
	villain	ˈvɪlən	Schuft, Schurke
	director	dəˈrektə	Regisseur
	to rehearse	tə rɪˈhɜːs	proben, einstudieren
	clearly	ˈklɪəlɪ	klar, eindeutig
	ghost	gəʊst	Geist, Gespenst
	feeling	ˈfiːlɪŋ	Gefühl, Empfindung
	line	laɪn	Zeile
	evil	ˈiːvl	übel, schlimm
	critic	ˈkrɪtɪk	Kritiker(in)
	to honour	tʊ ˈɒnə	ehren, hochschätzen, achten
	immortal	ɪˈmɔːtl	unsterblich
	ridiculous	rɪˈdɪkjələs	lächerlich, albern
	to shoot	tə ˈʃuːt	(er)schießen
	to rewrite	tə ˈriːˈraɪt	umschreiben
	musical	ˈmjuːzɪkl	musikalisch
43 H	dictionary	ˈdɪkʃnrɪ	Wörterbuch
43 J	measurement	ˈmeʒəmənt	Maßnahme
	negotiation	nɪgəʊʃɪˈeɪʃn	Verhandlung
43 K	dramatist	ˈdræmətɪst	Dramatiker
	tragedy	ˈtrædʒədɪ	Tragödie
	The Merry Wives of Windsor	ðə ˈmerɪ ˈwaɪvz əv ˈwɪnzə	Die lustigen Weiber von Windsor
	A Midsummer Night's Dream	ə ˈmɪdsʌmə naɪts ˈdriːm	Ein Sommernachtstraum
43 L	to be brought up	tə bɪ ˈbrɔːt ˈʌp	aufgezogen werden
	drama school	ˈdrɑːmə skuːl	Schauspielschule
43 M	motorbike	ˈməʊtəbaɪk	Motorrad
	eventually	ɪˈventʃʊəlɪ	schließlich, endlich
	cheerful	ˈtʃɪəfʊl	froh, freudig
	horrified	ˈhɒrɪfaɪd	entsetzt, schockiert
	criticism	ˈkrɪtɪsɪzm	Kritik

UNIT 44

Most doctors and dentists in Britain are self-employed, that is, they work for themselves. Most of the money they earn, however, comes from the National Health Service, which pays them according to the work they do for each patient. Almost all of them nowadays take private patients as well, who pay the full costs of their treatment and so avoid having to wait for checkups, hospital places, and so on. An ordinary family doctor is called a "G.P.", a general practitioner, and there is an increasing trend towards group practices, in which several doctors or dentists work together. Because there are so many English-speaking countries, a large number of British-trained doctors and dentists go abroad, for example to the United States, Australia or New Zealand, where they can earn more money.

44 A At the dentist's

(D = Dentist, J = Jane, R = Russell, A = Patient A, B = Patient B)

(Dentist's waiting-room)

D Good morning. I'm so sorry about the delay. But I'm on my own at the moment. My assistant has been held up. I've got a little job to finish, but I won't keep you long. It'll be done in no time.

J Charming man, isn't he?
A I've been told he's awful.
R Well, I do know one thing about him – he's slow.
I was told to come at nine.
I've been kept waiting an hour already.
I'm supposed to be back in my office by eleven.
A Are you? But you're being paid for all this waiting, I hope.
R Oh, I'm being paid all right. But we're having to check all our stock at the

R	moment. So we're being forced to work a lot of overtime, and they want me back as soon as possible.
J	I wonder if the crossword's been done yet. Ah no, it hasn't. Good. Does anyone know a five-letter word beginning with "t"?
R	What's the clue?
J	They're often pulled out.
B	Trees.
J	Right. Thank you very much.
R	I think the answer's "teeth". Teeth are pulled out much more often than trees.
J	Oh yes, that must be right.
A	Could I possibly have a look at the sports page? I'd like to see if Liverpool won.
J	It's been torn out. Oh – no. Wait a minute. Here it is. Er . . . Liverpool. No, they were beaten three nil by Brighton.
A	Oh. Thank you very much.
J	This crossword puzzle is too difficult for me.
R	Do you need any help?
J	Yes, I can't do this one. What language is spoken in Brazil?
R	Portuguese.
J	How is it spelt?
R	P – O –

	(noise of drilling)
J	What was that? What's going on in there?
A	Has he got a patient in there? If he has, he's being tortured.
B	Oh, I'm sure Mr Pullem wouldn't do that. He's said to be very good.
R	That's what I was told as well. He was recommended to me by a friend of mine.
J	Yes, I was recommended to come here by my doctor.
A	I was given his address by my father-in-law. He had all his teeth taken out by Mr Pullem.
B	He's supposed to be very good indeed.
R	Is he one of these modern dentists?
A	How do you mean?
R	You know – the kind where you listen to soft music while your teeth are being filled.
A	I don't know – I certainly hope not.
	(patient A lights a cigarette)
R	Er, you're not allowed to smoke here, by the way.
A	Oh, sorry. I didn't realise smoking was prohibited.
J	I still don't know how you spell Portuguese.
R	P – O – R – T –
	(noise of drill again)
A	Does he always make that noise?
B	Not normally. But there's no need to be worried. You can rely on him. I left my other dentist because he had a very pretty assistant and he kept talking to her while I was being treated. Doctor Pullem never does that. He's very thorough.
	(patient C leaves)
J	What's wrong with her?
R	She's been frightened away.

	(enter dentist)
D	Would you come in now, please?
A	Me? These people were before me. I wasn't told to come till twelve.
D	That doesn't matter, Mr Watson.
R	Well, I like that! He wasn't asked to come till twelve and now he's being treated first.

(voice from inside)

V	Ouch!
J	And by the sound of it he's being treated quite badly.
R	He hasn't been given an injection.

(noise again)

V	Agh! It's broken off!
J	I can't stand this any longer!
R	Neither can I.
J	Something has to be done.
R	He ought to be reported.
J	He'll be struck off the medical register.
B	I'm going in! I'm going to stop him!
D	I'm awfully sorry. I'll be finished in a moment. The drill has to be repaired before I can start.

44 B Questions

Where does the story take place?
Why does the dentist have to apologise?
What time should Russell be back in his office?
Why is he working overtime at the moment?
What is Jane doing while she's waiting?
One patient is interested in Jane's newspaper. Why?
What sort of noise can be heard from the dentist's room?
Why did one female patient leave the waiting-room?
What was the dentist repairing?

44 C And you?

Are you afraid of your dentist?
How often do you go to the dentist for a routine checkup?
What do you think about the dangers of smoking?
Give reasons for giving up smoking.

44 D The Passive (II)   Das Passiv

Continuous Form   **Verlaufsform**

present:	A tooth **is being pulled out**.	*Ein Zahn wird (gerade) gezogen.*	
	The house **is being painted**.	*Das Haus wird (gerade) gestrichen.*	
past:	A tooth **was being pulled out**.	*Ein Zahn wurde (gerade) gezogen.*	
	The house **was being painted**.	*Das Haus wurde (gerade) gestrichen.*	

Die Verlaufsform ist im Passiv nur für das Present und Past möglich. Sie wird mit "to be being" gebildet.

Man verwendet die Verlaufsform des Passivs, wenn ein Vorgang bezeichnet werden soll, der begonnen hat, aber noch nicht zu Ende ist, z. B.: The house was being built. *Das Haus wurde (gerade) gebaut.* Aber: The house was built. *Das Haus wurde gebaut.* (D. h., das vergangene passive Geschehen wird als abgeschlossene Tatsache erwähnt.)

44 E   Translate the sentences:

Ich glaube, wir werden beobachtet.
Die Zeitung wird gerade gedruckt.
Als ich in New York war, wurde das Museum of Modern Art gerade umgebaut. (to rebuild)
Viel Geld wird (zur Zeit) für Atomwaffen (nuclear weapons) ausgegeben.
Die Zimmer wurden eben sauber gemacht.
Wir werden (zur Zeit) gezwungen, Überstunden zu machen.
Ein Patient wird gerade behandelt.
Der Tee wird gerade serviert.

44 F   Persönliches Passiv

I was told to come at 9 o'clock.	*Man sagte mir, ich solle um 9 Uhr kommen.*
You are expected to work hard.	*Man erwartet von Ihnen, daß Sie hart arbeiten.*
He is said to be a good doctor.	*Er soll ein guter Arzt sein.*
She is supposed to be honest.	*Sie soll ehrlich sein. Sie gilt als ehrlich.*
I'm supposed to be there at 9 o'clock	*Ich soll um 9 Uhr dort sein.*

Mit dem Passiv drücken wir in unseren Beispielsätzen ein unbestimmtes Subjekt aus. Das Englische kann im Gegensatz zum Deutschen von einer weit größeren Zahl von Verben das persönliche Passiv bilden. Auch Verben, die eng mit einer Präposition verbunden sind, lassen ein persönliches Passiv zu, z. B.: They sent for the doctor. – The doctor was sent for. They'll look after the children. – The children will be looked after.
Englische Passivsätze dieser Art werden häufig im Deutschen mit dem unbestimmten Pronomen „man" wiedergegeben.

44 G   Translate the sentences, using the passive:

Man sagte mir, ich solle warten.
Welche Sprache spricht man in Brasilien?
Wie schreibt man das?
Er soll reich sein.
Man hat nie mehr wieder von ihm gehört.
Man sagte mir, er sei nach Amerika ausgewandert.
Man hörte dem Professor nicht zu.
Man hat mich nicht vom Bahnhof abgeholt. (to pick up)
Man hält sie für intelligent.

44 H Passivbildung mit zwei Objekten

		indirektes Objekt	direktes Objekt
Aktiv:	Somebody gave	her	a book.
Passiv:	indirektes Objekt als Subjekt:	She was given a book.	
	direktes Objekt als Subjekt:	A book was given to her.	

Eine kleine Gruppe wichtiger Verben, z. B. bring, give, show, tell kann ein indirektes und ein direktes Objekt haben. Da im Englischen beinahe jedes Objekt zum Subjekt eines Passivsatzes werden kann, ergeben sich bei diesen Verben zwei Möglichkeiten der Passivbildung. Die Konstruktion mit dem indirekten Objekt ist häufiger, eleganter und ganz typisch englisch: She was given a book.

44 I Rewrite the sentences in the passive:

They've frightened her away.
They'll tell us the news.
Someone showed her round.
They asked her some questions.
They promised the workers higher wages.

Someone promised him a tip.
She tells the children a story.
He's teaching us English.
He's just given her a present.

44 J Übersetzung von „werden"

shall/will + Infinitiv	I won't come.	*Ich werde nicht kommen.*
will be	He'll be forty next year.	*Er wird nächstes Jahr vierzig.*
to get	The lessons are getting more difficult.	*Die Lektionen werden schwieriger.*
to become	My brother became a dentist.	*Mein Bruder wurde Zahnarzt.*
to grow	It began to grow dark.	*Es begann dunkel zu werden.*
to turn	His hair turned grey.	*Seine Haare wurden grau.*
to go	Ophelia went mad when she lost Hamlet's love.	*Ophelia wurde wahnsinnig, als sie Hamlets Liebe verlor.*

44 K Vocabulary Practice

Explain the meaning of the expressions underlined:

It'll be done in no time.
We're having to check our stock.

He can't stand this any longer.
He ought to be reported.

44 L Find out the relationship

What do you call these relatives?

Your sister's husband is your …
Your mother's brother is your …
Your father's sister is your …
Your husband's sister is your …
Your husband's parents are your …

Your sister's son is your …
Your aunt's son is your …
Your mother's parents are your …
You are your husband's …
Your son is your mother's …

44 M The Welfare State (CB)

National Insurance

It is compulsory for all who have left school and go to work. It provides for sickness and unemployment benefits as well as old-age pensions.

National Health Service

It provides free medical services and prescriptions. The NHS covers hospital, medical and dental services.

National Assistance

It provides that any person over 16 can get financial help through the local National Assistance Board.

Family Allowances

They provide assistance for families with three or more children.

Are there similar institutions in your country?

44 N Situation – Say it in English

Lassen Sie sich bei einem Zahnarzt einen Termin geben.
Sagen Sie, daß Sie Zahnschmerzen haben.
Sie werden gefragt, welcher Zahn Ihnen weh tut.
Bitten Sie Ihren Zahnarzt, Ihnen eine Spritze zu geben.
Fragen Sie Ihren Gesprächspartner, ob es nicht besser wäre, wenn er zum Arzt ginge.
Sagen Sie, daß Sie Dr. X empfehlen würden.
Sagen Sie, daß Ihr kleiner Sohn Angst vor dem Zahnarzt hat.
Sagen Sie, daß Sie sich Sorgen über die Zukunft machen.
Wünschen Sie jemandem gute Besserung.

44 O Summary

There were five nervous patients in the waiting-room outside Dr Pullem's dental surgery. The dentist came in to say he was very sorry they were being kept waiting, but he was on his own as his assistant had been delayed.
The patients talked about Dr Pullem – Russell said he was slow, and another patient said he'd been told he was awful. Jane started to do the crossword in the paper while she was waiting, but

she wasn't very good at it, and the other patients had to help her. Suddenly there was an awful noise of drilling from the surgery – it sounded as if someone was being tortured. The patients went on talking about Dr Pullem. Russell wanted to know if he was one of those modern dentists who made you listen to music while your teeth were being filled, and another man said he had been given Dr Pullem's address by his father-in-law, who had had all his teeth taken out by Dr Pullem. Then the terrible noise started again, and Dr Pullem came and asked one of the patients to come in. Russell was very annoyed at this, as he'd been there longer. The noise started again, and got so bad that eventually the patients decided to go into the surgery – and found that no one was being tortured – the patient was helping Dr Pullem repair his drill!

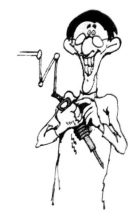

Prevention is better than cure

44

Vocabulary / Wortschatz

44	dentist	ˈdentɪst	Zahnarzt, Zahnärztin
	self-employed	ˈself ɪmˈplɔɪd	selbständig
	checkup	ˈtʃekʌp	gründliche Untersuchung
	general practitioner	ˈdʒenrəl prækˈtɪʃnə	Arzt für Allgemeinmedizin
	trend	trend	Tendenz
	towards	təˈwɔːdz	hin . . . zu
	group practices	ˈgruːp præktɪsɪz	Gemeinschaftspraxen
	to go abroad	tə gəʊ əˈbrɔːd	ins Ausland gehen
44 A	to hold, held, held up	tə həʊld, held ˈʌp	aufhalten
	I won't keep you long	aɪ ˈwəʊnt kiːp jʊ ˈlɒŋ	ich werde Sie nicht lange warten lassen
	in no time	ɪn ˈnəʊ taɪm	im Nu, sofort
	stock	stɒk	Lager, Warenbestand
	to be forced	tə bɪ ˈfɔːst	gezwungen sein
	to work overtime	tə ˈwɜːk ˈəʊvətaɪm	Überstunden machen
	crossword (puzzle)	ˈkrɒswɜːd (pʌzl)	Kreuzworträtsel
	clue	kluː	Anhaltspunkt, roter Faden, Schlüssel
	to pull out	tə pʊl ˈaʊt	herausreißen
	tooth, pl teeth	tuːθ, tiːθ	Zahn, Zähne
	to beat, beat, beaten	tə biːt, ˈbiːtn	schlagen
	nil	nɪl	null *(Sport)*
	Brazil	brəˈzɪl	Brasilien
	Portuguese	pɔːtjʊˈgiːz	portugiesisch; Portugiese, Portugiesin
	to drill	tə ˈdrɪl	bohren
	to torture	tə ˈtɔːtʃə	quälen, foltern

	father-in-law	ˈfɑːðərɪnlɔː	Schwiegervater
	soft	sɒft	leise, weich, zärtlich
	to light a cigarette	tə ˈlaɪt ə sɪgəˈret	eine Zigarette anzünden
	to prohibit	tə prəˈhɪbɪt	verbieten
	drill	drɪl	Bohrer, Bohrmaschine
	to treat	tə ˈtriːt	behandeln
	thorough	ˈθʌrə	gründlich
	to be frightened away	tə bɪ ˈfraɪtnd əˈweɪ	vertrieben, abgeschreckt werden
	ouch	aʊtʃ	au! autsch!
	sound	saʊnd	Ton, Klang, Geräusch
	injection	ɪnˈdʒekʃn	Spritze
	neither	naɪðə	auch nicht
	to report	tə rɪˈpɔːt	melden, anzeigen
	medical register	ˈmedɪkl ˈredʒɪstə	Ärzteliste, -register
44 B	female	ˈfiːmeɪl	weiblich
44 C	routine	ruːˈtiːn	routinemäßig
44 E	to rebuild	tə ˈriːˈbɪld	umbauen
	nuclear weapons	ˈnjuːklɪə ˈwepənz	Atomwaffen
44 G	to pick up	tə pɪk ˈʌp	abholen
	intelligent	ɪnˈtelɪdʒənt	intelligent, klug
44 I	wages	ˈweɪdʒɪz	Löhne
44 L	sister-in-law	ˈsɪstərɪnlɔː	Schwägerin
	parents-in-law	ˈpeərəntsɪnlɔː	Schwiegereltern
	grandparents	ˈgrændpeərənts	Großeltern
44 M	welfare	ˈwelfeə	Wohlfahrt, Fürsorge
	insurance	ɪnˈʃʊərəns	Versicherung
	compulsory	kəmˈpʌlsərɪ	obligatorisch, zwingend
	to provide	tə prəˈvaɪd	vorsehen
	sickness	sɪknəs	Krankheit
	unemployment benefit	ʌnɪmˈplɔɪmənt ˈbenɪfɪt	Arbeitslosenunterstützung
	old-age pension	ˈəʊld eɪdʒ ˈpenʃn	Pension, Altersruhegeld
	National Assistance Board	ˈnæʃnəl əˈsɪstəns bɔːd	öffentliche Fürsorge
	allowance	əˈlaʊəns	Zuschuß, Beihilfe, Unterstützung
44 N	toothache	ˈtuːθeɪk	Zahnschmerzen
44 O	dental surgery	ˈdentl ˈsɜːdʒərɪ	Zahnarzt-Praxis
	to be annoyed	tə bɪ əˈnɔɪd	sich ärgern, verärgert sein
	Prevention is better than cure	prɪˈvenʃn ɪz betə ðn ˈkjʊə	Vorbeugen ist besser als heilen

UNIT 45

Lincoln's Inn – one of the four Inns of Court

The area around the Royal Courts of Justice is sometimes called "Legal London" – it's the centre of the legal system in England (not Britain, because there are two quite separate systems of law in Britain). Scottish law is completely different from English law and has its headquarters in Edinburgh.

The four Inns of Court are called Lincoln's Inn, the Inner Temple, the Middle Temple, and Gray's Inn. They're colleges of barristers and law students and they're all about 500 years old. Originally the Inns were actually inns – places where lawyers and law students could live and eat.

The Old Bailey is one of the most famous criminal courts in the world. It's near St. Paul's Cathedral. Many famous murder trials were held there. The Old Bailey stands on the site of the old Newgate Prison, which was demolished in 1902. Many famous people, such as Daniel Defoe, the author of *Robinson Crusoe*, were imprisoned there.

45 A The new sports car

(R = Russell, J = Jane, T = Tomkins)

(Anteroom of a court, Jane and Russell are barristers, Tomkins is Russell's pupil)

R Thank goodness.
   What a difficult case this is!
   I needed the break.
J So did I.
   It's so stuffy in that courtroom.
R It's always the same with this judge.
   He always has the windows closed.
   He's afraid of catching a cold.
J How about going to the dining-hall for a bite to eat?
R I've got an appointment at twelve.
   But we can have lunch together.
J Lovely.

55

R	Tomkins! Where's Tomkins?
J	Who's Tomkins?
R	He's my new pupil. He's a bit slow, you know. Ah, there you are, Tomkins. I wish you wouldn't keep me waiting.
T	Sorry, Mr Grant.
R	Well, we were thinking of going over to lunch in a moment. Would you like to join us?
T	Thank you for asking, Mr Grant, but could I have a word with you for a moment?
R	Is it about the case?
T	No, it's a private matter, Mr Grant.
R	Some other time, Tomkins.
T	But I'd like to apologise for . . .
R	Tomkins, would you mind putting these papers away?
R	Cigarette?
J	No, thank you. I don't smoke.
R	Tomkins?
T	No, thank you. I've given up smoking.
R	Have you?
T	Yes, I'm saving up for a new car. I can't afford to spend so much on smoking.
R	Ah, a new car, eh? I've just bought a new car. It's parked outside in Lincoln's Inn Fields.
J	What colour is it?
T	It's red, isn't it, Mr Grant?
R	How did you know?
T	I saw a big red car parked in Lincoln's Inn Fields.
R	Yes, that's mine.
T	I knew it was his.
J	Is it a sports car?
R	Yes, it's the new GT5. It does a hundred and twenty.
J	You enjoy driving fast, don't you?
R	Yes, I do.
J	But surely it's dangerous and very expensive.
R	No, it isn't. Of course you have to be careful with overtaking and so on. The car is quite small, so it's convenient for parking in London. I never have any problems now with parking.
T	I do. Parking a car is the most difficult thing of all.
R	It's a great advantage having a fast car. I handle a lot of Scottish cases. So it's very good for going up to Edinburgh.
J	But it's not a very good car for shopping, I imagine.

T	Excuse me interrupting you, Mr Grant.
R	Yes, Tomkins, what is it?
T	That private matter I mentioned . . .
R	Some other time, Tomkins. Don't you remember my saying that?
T	Yes, I do, but . . .
R	Now, no buts, Tomkins. Go and answer the telephone, will you?
J	Poor Tomkins! You're hard on him.
R	Yes, I believe in being hard on pupils. It's the best way of teaching them.

R	He's a good fellow, but I can't stand his interrupting me all the time.	T	Thank you, Mr Grant.
		R	Is that all, Tomkins?
J	But I think he wants to tell you something. Why don't you ask him what's on his mind?	T	No, not quite, Mr Grant. You see, while I was parking my car this morning, I hit another car without meaning to.
R	All right, perhaps I will.		
		R	Oh, hard luck, Tomkins.
T	There's somebody waiting to see you downstairs, Mr Grant.	J	Was there any damage?
		T	Well, my car is perfectly all right.
R	Thank you, Tomkins. I'll be down in a minute. But tell me Tomkins, what's troubling you?	R	Then stop worrying.
		T	But the other car's got a few scratches.
		R	Really, Tomkins. All this fuss about a few scratches? I'm sure the owner won't mind.
T	Well, it's like this, Mr Grant. I'd like to apologise for parking so badly this morning.		
		T	I'm afraid he will.
		R	What do you mean?
R	What do you mean, Tomkins?	T	Well, you see, it's the big red sports car in Lincoln's Inn Fields. You're the owner.
T	I'm no good at parking.		
R	But you can't be good at everything. You're very good at your job.		

45

45 B Questions

What's the name of the famous criminal court in London?
Who was Daniel Defoe?
Can you explain the expression "Inns of Court"?
Who is Tomkins in our story?

Why did Tomkins want to speak to Mr Grant?
Why has Tomkins given up smoking?
Russell's new sports car does a hundred and twenty.
How many kilometres are 120 miles?

45 C And you?

Are you good at parking?
Have you ever been inside a court?
Have you ever been involved in a legal matter?
Have you ever paid a fine?

45 D The ing-form (III)

after adjective + preposition

Die ing-Form

nach Adjektiv + Präposition

He's **afraid of catching** a cold.	*Er hat Angst, sich zu erkälten.*
I'm no **good at parking.**	*Ich bin nicht gut im Einparken.*
Of course you have to be **careful with overtaking.**	*Natürlich muß man beim Überholen vorsichtig sein.*

Weitere Beispiele für die Verbindung Adjektiv + Präposition:

accustomed to	*gewöhnt an*
astonished at	*erstaunt über*
engaged in	*beschäftigt mit*
famous for	*berühmt für*
fond of	*gerne tun, mögen*
glad about	*erfreut über*
happy about	*glücklich über*
interested in	*interessiert an*
keen on	*erpicht auf*
proud of	*stolz auf*
responsible for	*verantwortlich für*
tired of	*(einer Sache) müde sein, (etw.) satt haben*
used to	*gewöhnt an*

45 E Complete the sentences with the correct preposition + ing-form:

He's no good ... money. (make)
She was afraid ... her way. (lose)
I'm tired ... your questions. (answer)
He couldn't get accustomed ... late. (work)
Jane's fond ... (dance).
He was responsible ... the meeting. (prepare)
Would you be interested ... me about it? (tell)
The actors were happy ... for us. (work)
Are you keen ...? (travel)

45 F The ing-form   **Die ing-Form**

after noun + preposition   **nach Substantiv + Präposition**

Do you think there's any **chance of getting** a job? *Glauben Sie, daß es überhaupt eine Chance gibt, eine Stelle zu bekommen?*
It's the best **method of teaching.** *Es ist die beste Methode zu unterrichten.*

Weitere Beispiele für die Verbindung Substantiv + Präposition:

danger of	*Gefahr ... zu, daß*
difficulty (in, of)	*Schwierigkeit ... zu*
dislike for (of)	*Abneigung ... zu, gegen*
experience in	*Erfahrung in*
habit of	*Gewohnheit ... zu*
interest in	*Interesse an*
love for	*Vorliebe, Neigung ... zu*
opportunity of	*Gelegenheit ... zu*
pleasure of (in)	*Vergnügen, Freude ... zu*
reason for	*Grund ... zu, für*
risk of (in)	*Risiko ... zu*
way of	*Art und Weise ... zu*

Bei einigen Verbindungen kann die Präposition wechseln oder sogar wegfallen, z. B.:
The difficulty of finding a job. Aber: I had some difficulty (in) finding a job.

45 G Translate the sentences: ○○

Ich bin sicher, es wird Ihnen bald gelingen, gut Englisch zu sprechen.
Sie werden keine Schwierigkeiten haben, die Prüfung zu bestehen.
Es bestand keine Gefahr, den (Rechts-)Fall zu verlieren.
Ich denke, er fürchtet angeklagt zu werden. (to accuse)
Er kann seine Gewohnheit, vor dem Frühstück zu rauchen, nicht ändern.
Ich habe keinen Grund, Ihnen das zu erzählen.
Wir freuen uns, Ihnen den Auftrag bestätigen (to acknowledge) zu können.
Es hat keinen Sinn, sich jetzt zu beschweren.
Ich denke, daß es nichts bringt, ihm zu schreiben.
Verzeihen Sie, wenn ich Sie störe.

45 H The ing-form after prepositions   Die ing-Form nach Präpositionen

Tomkins hit another car **without meaning** to.	*... ohne es zu wollen*
We got the job finished **by working** twelve hours a day.	*... dadurch, daß wir arbeiteten*
She's always preferred making her own clothes **instead of buying** them in the shops.	*... (an)statt zu kaufen*

Nach alleinstehenden Präpositionen steht die ing-Form. Im Deutschen steht hier der Infinitiv oder ein Nebensatz.

45 I Underline the stressed syllable of the following words:

difficult – courtroom – dining-hall – together – pupil – moment – matter – apologise – afford – dangerous – expensive – advantage – Edinburgh – remember – something – fellow – downstairs – perfectly – morning – owner

45 J Find opposites to the following adjectives:

careful – slow – expensive – big – difficult – private

Make sentences with each opposite.

45 K A message

I'd like to apologise for damaging your car this morning. It was entirely my fault – I drove into the parking space without looking. Here's my name and address: Nicholas Patten, 16 St. George's Road, London SW3 Tel: (01) 346 72284. My insurance company is: Standard Vehicle Insurance Company Ltd., Swan Buildings, Chelmsford, Essex (Insurance No. JE 35829066 E)

P. S. Sorry!

45 L Situation – Say it in English

Sie haben etwas nicht verstanden. Fragen Sie Ihren Gesprächspartner, wie er das meint.
Fragen Sie ihn, worauf er hinauswill.
Fragen Sie ihn, ob er nicht ein wenig zu streng mit seinen Kindern ist.
Fragen Sie einen Freund, ob Sie kurz mit ihm sprechen könnten.
Ihr Freund möchte wissen, was Sie auf dem Herzen haben.
Schlagen Sie Ihrem Gesprächspartner vor, in den Speisesaal zu gehen
und eine Kleinigkeit zu essen.
Sagen Sie, daß Sie es nicht leiden können, ständig unterbrochen zu werden.

45 M Summary

This time Jane and Russell were barristers who were working together on a very difficult case. During a break, Jane suggested going to the dining-hall for lunch. First, though, Russell called Tomkins, his new pupil, who was a bit slow – he wanted to ask him to join them. But Tomkins delayed them by asking if he could talk to Russell about a private matter. Russell said this wasn't the right time to discuss things like that. Russell offered Tomkins a cigarette, but Tomkins said he'd given up smoking, as he was saving up for a new car. Russell started talking about his new car, a red GT5 sports car. Jane said a fast car like that must be expensive and dangerous, but Russell said it was very useful for going up to Scotland. Tomkins kept trying to talk to Russell, but Russell sent him away to answer the phone.

When he came back, Russell asked him what the matter was. Tomkins said he wasn't very good at parking, and had hit another car while he was parking his car in Lincoln's Inn Fields that morning. Russell said he was sure the owner wouldn't mind a few scratches – but Tomkins said it was Russell's new sports car!

Easy come, easy go

Vocabulary — Wortschatz

45	court of justice	ˈkɔːt əv ˈdʒʌstɪs	Gerichtshof
	justice	ˈdʒʌstɪs	Gerechtigkeit; Rechtmäßigkeit; Gerichtsbarkeit
	legal	ˈliːgəl	gesetzlich, Gesetz-; rechtmäßig, Rechts-
	Inns of Court	ˈɪnz əv ˈkɔːt	(die vier Londoner) Rechtsschulen
	inn	ɪn	Gast-, Wirtshaus
	barrister	ˈbærɪstə	vor Gericht plädierender Anwalt
	law student	ˈlɔː stjuːdnt	Student der Rechtswissenschaften
	lawyer	ˈlɔɪə	Jurist, Rechtsanwalt
	Old Bailey	ˈəʊld ˈbeɪlɪ	Londoner Schwurgericht
	criminal court	ˈkrɪmɪnl ˈkɔːt	Strafkammer
	murder trial	ˈmɜːdə traɪəl	Mordprozeß
	to demolish	tə dɪˈmɒlɪʃ	abreißen, zertrümmern, zerstören
45 A	anteroom	ˈæntɪruːm	Vorzimmer
	break	breɪk	Pause, Unterbrechung
	stuffy	ˈstʌfɪ	stickig
	judge	dʒʌdʒ	Richter
	dining-hall	ˈdaɪnɪŋ hɔːl	Speisesaal
	bite	baɪt	Imbiß
	colour	ˈkʌlə	Farbe
	to overtake	tʊ əʊvəˈteɪk	überholen

	fellow	ˈfeləʊ	Kamerad, Bursche, Kerl, Kumpel
	mind	maɪnd	Kopf, Geist, Denkweise
	damage	ˈdæmɪdʒ	Schaden
	scratch	skrætʃ	Kratzer, Schramme
45 B	to originate	tʊ əˈrɪdʒəneɪt	entstehen, anfangen
	meal	miːl	Mahlzeit
45 C	involved in	ɪnˈvɒlvd ɪn	(hinein)verwickelt
	fine	faɪn	(Geld-)Strafe
45 D	accustomed to	əˈkʌstəmd tə	gewöhnt an
	astonished at	əˈstɒnɪʃt ət	erstaunt über
	fond of	ˈfɒnd əv	gerne tun, mögen
	keen on	ˈkiːn ɒn	erpicht auf
	proud of	ˈpraʊd əv	stolz auf
45 E	to dance	tə ˈdɑːns	tanzen
45 F	habit	ˈhæbɪt	Gewohnheit
	opportunity	ɒpəˈtjuːnəti	Gelegenheit
	risk	rɪsk	Risiko
	way	weɪ	Art und Weise
45 G	to accuse	tʊ əˈkjuːz	anschuldigen, anklagen
	to acknowledge	tʊ əkˈnɒlɪdʒ	bestätigen
45 K	entirely	ɪnˈtaɪəlɪ	gänzlich, einzig und allein, ausschließlich
45 L	to aim at	tʊ ˈeɪm ət	abzielen auf, auf etwas hinauswollen
45 M	Easy come, easy go	ˈiːzɪ ˈkʌm, ˈiːzɪ ˈgəʊ	Wie gewonnen, so zerronnen

UNIT 46

(CB) Britain's economic difficulties are mainly the result of the great change in Britain's role since the Second World War. For about 200 years, from the early 18th to the early 20th century, Britain was the richest country in the world, and until just after the Second World War it ruled the largest empire the world has ever seen. The territories of the British Empire were an enormous market for British products, and supplied Britain with cheap raw materials. In the thirty years following World War II Britain gave independence to all its major overseas territories and so lost its cheap raw materials and easy markets, since the governments of the newly independent Commonwealth countries were free to trade exactly as they wished. So Britain had to begin to compete seriously with other countries for the first time. And a new problem arose. In the 19th century Britain had the most modern industry in the world, but the factories built in the 19th century were not able to change quickly to meet the new conditions after the War, and failed to make a profit. For several decades after World War II, the British economy recorded weak growth and was sometimes referred to as the "sick man of Europe". However since 1992 Britain has seen a long period of sustained economic growth. It is nowadays one of the strongest economies in the European Union.

46 A Going on strike 🎧

(B = Boss, R = Russell, J = Jane, F = Fred, M = Maisie, Bill)

(Factory office, boss's door half open)

B Hello.
   Ah, Jack, good morning.
   Have you been terribly busy all morning? I asked you to ring me back. I wanted to talk to you about my ideas for making the factory more efficient. We must above all try not to waste time. I've decided to stop this morning teabreak from today. I'd like to see if I can do without it. And then another very important thing is – we must make sure . . .

(scene changes to Russell and other workers)

R Where's the shop steward? Jane!
J Yes, what's the matter?
R Listen to this.
   He's decided to stop our teabreak.
J What?
   Stop our teabreak? Who?
R Him. The boss. Our teabreak.
   He wants to stop it.
J How do you know?
R I heard him say it on the phone.
   What can we do about it?
J We must go on strike.

R Look at him talking.
   He's talking about our teabreak.

(boss's office)

B Why pay more? Why not make an agreement on a new system for arranging . . .
   Just a moment.
   I must close the door.
   There's such a noise outside.

R I saw him shut the door.
   He didn't want us to hear.
J Right. Down tools, everybody.
   Come over here.
F What's the matter now?
J We're going on strike.
R Hey, Bill. Stop working.
Bill What for?
   What's going on?
J We're on strike.
Bill Oh, lovely.
   What is it this time?
J He's decided to stop our teabreak.
Bill Our teabreak?
   He can't do that.
J You're right. We can't let him get away with that.

(Maisie comes with tea trolley)

R What would Maisie do then?
M I'd be out of a job.
R Quick. Have a cup of tea before the boss comes in and stops us.
F But I've got my tea.
J But he wants to stop it.
F Ah, now I'm beginning to understand.
   He wants us to bring our own tea.
R No, Fred. No tea, none at all.
F But he can't do that.
J That's what we've been telling you.
   Right, brothers.

J	We've got a right to a half-hour teabreak. We negotiated it last year. This is a matter of principle. We're going on strike until it's settled.
F	I'm not sure about a strike, though. We'd better call a Union meeting, hadn't we?
J	Yes, we must call a general meeting. But what we need is a lightning strike first to make him change his mind.
	(boss's office)
B	No, no. I won't regret it. I don't intend to change my mind. I'd like to see if I can do without a teabreak. The workers can drink all the tea they want. It keeps them happy. But I just can't afford the time for a teabreak every day. And we managers must set a good example.

(workers with placards)

J	Remember to do what I said.
J	We all march in there and tell him what we think. We'll make him change his mind. Everybody ready? *(placards: "Hands off our teabreak", "We want action – hands off our jobs", "We want more tea")*
Others	Yes, we're ready.
J	Where's your placard?
M	I took it home after the demonstration last week. I forgot to bring it back.
J	Bill, what's that supposed to mean? We don't want more tea – we just want tea.
Bill	Oh, I see. Tea!
J	This is a strike about our teabreak. Come on. Let's go.
	(boss's office)
B	Wait a minute. There's something going on. I'll ring you back. What's all this? What's going on here? "Hands off our jobs", "We want more tea".
J	No, we don't want more tea. Just tea.
B	I fail to understand.
R	I heard you say it.
B	Heard me say what?
R	You've decided to stop our teabreak.
B	So that's it. Mr Grant, if you must listen to my telephone calls, remember to listen more carefully.
R	What do you mean?
B	I don't intend to stop your teabreak, Mr Grant. I'm only stopping mine.

46 B Questions

When did Britain join the Common Market?
Why do workers normally go on strike?
Who did the boss talk to on the phone in our story?
What is Jane's job?
What did Russell hear?
What sort of strike did the workers agree to?
What do they intend to do later?

46 C And you?

Do people often go on strike in your country?
Do you think working conditions have improved during the last few years?
Which country has got a higher rate of unemployment – Britain or the country where you live?
How does industry spoil the countryside?
What articles does your country import from Britain?

46 D to-infinitive   Infinitiv mit "to"

a) after certain verbs   nach bestimmten Verben

He has decided to stop our teabreak.	*Er hat beschlossen, unsere Teepause einzustellen.*
I don't intend to change my mind.	*Ich habe nicht vor, meine Meinung zu ändern.*
I fail to understand.	*Ich verstehe nicht. (Ich begreife nicht.)*

In diesen Beispielsätzen hat die Handlung, die mit dem to-infinitive beschrieben wird, dasselbe Subjekt wie das Verb, von dem der to-infinitive abhängt.

Weitere wichtige Verben, nach denen der to-infinitive verwendet wird:

agree, arrange, ask, expect, forget, happen, hope, learn, manage, offer, prepare, promise, refuse, try, wish.

Nach den Verben begin, continue, hate, like, love, prefer und start kann sowohl der to-infinitive als auch die ing-Form stehen.

b) after adjectives   nach Adjektiven

It's nice to have a helpful neighbour.	*Es ist schön, einen hilfsbereiten Nachbarn zu haben.*
It's not difficult to learn English.	*Es ist nicht schwierig, Englisch zu lernen.*
She was pleased to meet him.	*Sie freute sich, ihn zu treffen.*

c) after "what", "where", "when", "which", "how"

| I've no idea what to do and where to go. | *Ich habe keine Ahnung, was ich tun soll und wohin ich gehen soll.* |
| I don't know how to pronounce the name of that place. | *Ich weiß nicht, wie man den Namen dieses Ortes ausspricht.* |

46 E Object + to-infinitive — Objekt + Infinitiv mit "to"

He wants us to bring our own tea.	*Er will, daß wir den Tee selbst mitbringen.*
I asked you to ring me back.	*Ich bat Sie, mich zurückzurufen.*
I'll remind you to take your sunglasses.	*Ich werde Sie daran erinnern, Ihre Sonnenbrille mitzunehmen.*
She helps her to clean the house.	*Sie hilft ihr, das Haus sauberzumachen.*
Would you like me to help you?	*Möchten Sie, daß ich Ihnen helfe?*

Die Handlung, die mit dem to-infinitive beschrieben wird, hat hier nicht dasselbe Subjekt wie das Verb, von dem der to-infinitive abhängig ist. Diese Konstruktion besitzt im Deutschen oft keine direkte Entsprechung und wird daher häufig mit einem „daß"-Satz wiedergegeben.

46 F Infinitive without "to" — Infinitiv ohne "to"

I must go now.	*Ich muß jetzt gehen.*
We'd better call a meeting.	*Es wäre besser, eine Versammlung einzuberufen.*
I'd rather do it myself.	*Ich möchte es lieber selber machen.*
Why pay more at other shops?	*Warum sollen wir in anderen Geschäften mehr bezahlen?*
Why not make an agreement?	*Warum schließen wir kein Abkommen?*

Den Infinitiv ohne "to" finden wir nach unvollständigen Hilfsverben und nach den Ausdrücken "had better" und "would rather".
"Why" + Infinitiv ohne "to" deutet darauf hin, daß eine Handlung unnötig oder sinnlos ist. Mit "why not" + Infinitiv ohne "to" machen wir Vorschläge.

46 G Object + infinitive without "to"

I saw him shut the door.	*Ich sah, daß er die Tür zumachte.*
I heard you say it.	*Ich hörte, daß Sie es sagten.*
We can't let him get away with that.	*Wir können es nicht zulassen, daß er ungeschoren davonkommt.*
We'll make him change his mind.	*Wir werden dafür sorgen, daß er seine Meinung ändert.*

Die Konstruktion Objekt + Infinitiv ohne "to" finden wir nach den Verben der Wahrnehmung wie z. B. "see, watch, hear, feel, notice, listen to" sowie nach "let" und "have" im Sinne von *veranlassen* und nach "make". (Vgl. auch 50 F)

46 H to-infinitive or infinitive without "to"?

You'd better ... her yourself. (tell)
He promised ... (come)
I advise you ... in bed. (stay)
I'll let you ... as soon as possible. (know)
Did anyone notice the thief ... the house? (leave)
We'd rather ... home. (go)
I saw her ... the road when the lights were red. (cross)
We asked the mail order firm ... us the catalogue. (send)
They invited me ... my holidays at their home. (spend)
Mr Benson watched them ... for the play. (rehearse)
He refuses ... a higher rent. (pay)
We managed ... the train. (catch)

46 I Use the following idiomatic phrases in sentences:

- make up one's mind
- do one's best
- take care of
- on business
- look forward to

- have a nice time
- pass a test
- make a mistake
- catch a cold
- go for a walk

46 J Business letters

Placing an order

>   John Reed
>   25 Milk Street
>   Truro, Cornwall
>
> 2 July 19 . .
> Jonathan Kenny Ltd.
> 139 Elm Park Mansions
> Park Walk
> London EC1E 4BQ
>
> Dear Sirs
>
> I wish to order two sets of tea-towels as advertised in this month's "Greenwich Magazine".
> I enclose a postal order for £11.50 to cover purchase, postage and packing.
>
> Yours faithfully
> John Reed

Can you acknowledge the order?

46 K Trade Unions (CB)

Since the factory system had so much weakened the position of the individual worker during the Industrial Revolution, there was a trend in the early 19th century to form associations to protect the interests of workers. These associations were called trade unions. In 1868 a central federation of all British trade unions was founded in Manchester called the Trades Union Congress (T.U.C.). The unions' main task is to fight for higher wages and to improve the workers' standard of living. The British trade unions were closely linked with political action. It was therefore largely due to their activities that the Labour Party was created.

The members of a union have to pay subscriptions. In return they get strike pay if necessary. Some enterprises have adopted the "closed shop" which means that only union members are to be employed.

46 L Comment

Write a short comment on one of the following subjects.

Should trade unions be involved in politics?
Trade unions in your country.

46 M Charles Dickens (1812–1870) (CB)

Dickens was born into a poor family. At the age of twelve he was sent to work at a factory. At the age of fifteen, he entered a solicitor's office as a junior clerk. Three years later he became a newspaper reporter and wrote his first sketches. Within a few years he had become a very popular novelist. In many of his novels he described the bitter years of his childhood. In *Oliver Twist* and *David Copperfield* he wrote about the lives of the poor during the Victorian age. He also wrote *Pickwick Papers* and *Great Expectations*, as well as the well-known Christmas story *A Christmas Carol*. He died in 1870 and is buried in Poets' Corner in Westminster Abbey.

46 N Situation – Say it in English

Sagen Sie, daß Sie sich entschlossen haben, diesen Sommer zu Hause zu bleiben.
Sagen Sie, daß Sie es sich nicht leisten können, wegzufahren.
Sagen Sie, daß es Ihnen nichts ausmacht, in der Stadt zu bleiben.
Sagen Sie, daß die Lebenshaltungskosten immer teurer werden und
die Einkommen immer niedriger.
Ihr Gesprächspartner gibt Ihnen in diesem Punkt recht.
Fragen Sie Ihren Gesprächspartner, was Sie (1. Pers. Pl.) dagegen unternehmen können.

46 O Summary

The factory boss was talking to a friend on the phone about his plans for making the factory more efficient. He said it was important not to waste time, so he was stopping the morning teabreak at once. Russell, a worker in the factory, overheard him, and immediately called Jane, the shop steward. They watched the boss talking for a bit, then Jane said they should go on strike to make him change his mind – after all, if he stopped their teabreak, Maisie, the tea-girl, would lose her job. So they decided to have a lightning strike. But they didn't hear the boss explain whose teabreak he was intending to stop. They went into his office with placards saying "Hands off our teabreak", but the boss told them he didn't intend to stop their teabreak, only his own!

No pains, no gains

Vocabulary   **Wortschatz**

46			
	role	rəʊl	Rolle
	empire	ˈempaɪə	Reich
	market	ˈmɑːkɪt	Markt
	to supply	tə səˈplaɪ	(be)liefern
	raw material	ˈrɔː məˈtɪərɪəl	Rohstoff
	the major overseas territories	ðə ˈmeɪdʒər əʊvəsiːz ˈterɪtrɪz	die größten Überseegebiete
	easy markets	ˈiːzɪ ˈmɑːkɪts	billige Märkte
	Commonwealth countries	ˈkɒmənwelθ ˈkʌntrɪz	Länder des Commonwealth
	to trade	tə ˈtreɪd	Handel treiben
	to wish	tə ˈwɪʃ	wünschen, wollen
	to compete with	tə kəmˈpiːt wɪð	konkurrieren mit
	to arise, arose, arisen	tʊ əˈraɪz, əˈrəʊz, əˈrɪzn	auftauchen, entstehen, hervorkommen, hervorgehen
	factory	ˈfæktrɪ	Fabrik
	to fail	tə ˈfeɪl	seinen Zweck verfehlen, mißlingen, fehlschlagen
	they failed to make a profit	ðeɪ ˈfeɪld tə meɪk ə ˈprɒfɪt	sie erzielten keinen Gewinn

	to modernise	tə ˈmɒdənaɪz	modernisieren
	to bring down	tə brɪŋ ˈdaʊn	senken
	inflation	ɪnˈfleɪʃn	Inflation
46 A	efficient	ɪˈfɪʃnt	leistungsfähig, tüchtig
	teabreak	ˈtiːbreɪk	Teepause
	to make sure	tə meɪk ˈʃɔː	sicherstellen, klarstellen
	worker	ˈwɜːkə	Arbeiter(in)
	shop steward	ʃɒp ˈstjuːəd	Betriebsratsmitglied
	arrangement	əˈreɪndʒmənt	Vereinbarung, Abmachung
	we can't let him get away with that	wɪ ˈkɑːnt let ɪm get əweɪ wɪð ˈðæt	wir können es nicht zulassen, daß er ungeschoren davonkommt
	trolley	ˈtrɒlɪ	Handwagen
	to negotiate	tə nɪˈgəʊʃɪeɪt	aushandeln, verhandeln
	a matter of principle	ə ˈmætər əv prɪnsɪpl	eine Grundsatzfrage
	until it's settled	ənˈtɪl ɪts ˈsetld	bis es beigelegt ist
	union meeting	ˈjuːnjən ˈmiːtɪŋ	Gewerkschaftsversammlung
	general meeting	ˈdʒenrəl ˈmiːtɪŋ	Generalversammlung
	lightning strike	ˈlaɪtnɪŋ ˈstraɪk	Blitzstreik
	to change one's mind	tə ˈtʃeɪndʒ wʌnz ˈmaɪnd	seine Meinung ändern
	manager	ˈmænɪdʒə	Betriebsleiter, Direktor
	to set a good example	tə ˈset ə gʊd ɪgˈzɑːmpl	mit gutem Beispiel vorangehen
	placard	ˈplækɑːd	Plakat, Transparent
	to march in	tə mɑːtʃ ˈɪn	hineinmarschieren
	Hands off!	ˈhændz ˈɒf	Hände weg!
	demonstration	demənˈstreɪʃn	Kundgebung, Demonstration
	What's that supposed to mean?	wɒts ˈðæt səpəʊs tə miːn	Was soll das heißen?
	to ring back	tə rɪŋ ˈbæk	zurückrufen
	I fail to understand	aɪ ˈfeɪl tʊ ʌndəˈstænd	ich verstehe nicht
46 B	dissatisfied	dɪˈsætɪsfaɪd	unzufrieden
	conversation	kɒnvəˈseɪʃn	Unterhaltung, Gespräch
46 C	rate of unemployment	ˈreɪt əv ʌnɪmˈplɔɪmənt	Arbeitslosenrate, -quote
	to spoil	tə ˈspɔɪl	verderben
	countryside	ˈkʌntrɪsaɪd	Landschaft, Land
46 E	sunglasses	ˈsʌnglɑːsɪz	Sonnenbrille
46 I	to make up one's mind	tə meɪk ˈʌp wʌnz ˈmaɪnd	sich entschließen
46 J	a set of tea-towels	ə ˈset əv ˈtiː taʊəlz	ein Satz, eine Garnitur Geschirrtücher
	to enclose	tʊ ɪnˈkləʊz	beilegen, beifügen
	postal order	ˈpəʊstl ɔːdə	Postanweisung
	packing	ˈpækɪŋ	Verpackung
	receipt	rɪˈsiːt	Empfang, Erhalt
	to pass on an order	tə ˈpɑːs ɒn ən ɔːdə	einen Auftrag weiterleiten
	despatch department	dɪˈspætʃ dɪˈpɑːtmənt	Versandabteilung
	delivery	dɪˈlɪvərɪ	Lieferung

46 K	trade union	treɪd ˈjuːnjən	Gewerkschaft
	to weaken	tə ˈwiːkən	schwächen
	association	əsəʊsɪˈeɪʃn	Vereinigung
	Trades Union Congress	ˈtreɪdz ˈjuːnjən ˈkɒŋgres	Gewerkschafts-Kongreß
	task	tɑːsk	Aufgabe
	standard of living	ˈstændəd əv ˈlɪvɪŋ	Lebensstandard
	therefore	ˈðeəfɔː	deshalb, daher
	due to	ˈdjuː tə	infolge
	subscription	səbˈskrɪpʃn	Beitrag
	strike pay	ˈstraɪk peɪ	Streikgeld
	enterprise	ˈentəpraɪz	Unternehmen
	to adopt	tʊ əˈdɒpt	an-, aufnehmen
	closed shop	ˈkləʊzd ʃɒp	Betrieb, in dem nur Mitglieder einer bestimmten Gewerkschaft arbeiten
	to be employed	tə bɪ ɪmˈplɔɪd	(bei einer Firma) arbeiten
46 M	solicitor	səˈlɪsɪtə	(nicht plädierender) Rechtsanwalt
	junior clerk	ˈdʒuːnjə ˈklɑːk	Bürolehrling
	sketch	sketʃ	Skizze, Kurzgeschichte
	bitter	ˈbɪtə	bitter, schmerzlich, hart
	childhood	ˈtʃaɪldhʊd	Kindheit
	expectation	ekspekˈteɪʃn	Erwartung
46 O	to overhear	tʊ əʊvəˈhɪə	zufällig mithören, abhören, lauschen
	No pains, no gains	nəʊ peɪnz nəʊ geɪnz	Ohne Fleiß, kein Preis

UNIT 47

Polperro, Cornwall

Cornwall is the most southwesterly county in Britain. It is a long thin peninsula which ends at the rocky cliffs at Land's End, the last land before America as one travels westwards. Cornwall has the mildest climate of any part of Britain. The Gulf Stream warms its coasts, the dramatic rocky north coast with its high cliffs, and the gentle wooded south coast, so that palm trees and tropical plants grow in many places. For over two thousand years the main industry in Cornwall was tin mining, but now most of the mines are closed, and the landscape is full of their ruined engine-houses. About two hundred years ago, the mining of china-clay – used in making pottery – developed, and the area around St. Austell reminds one of a moon landscape with its pyramid-shaped china-clay tips.

Nowadays the most important industry in Cornwall is tourism. The ruins on the cliffs above Tintagel are a popular tourist attraction – King Arthur is said to have had his castle there. The stories of King Arthur and the Knights of the Round Table, which arose in Cornwall, gave rise to some of the most famous European romances, such as the story of Tristan and Isolde. Cornwall is also famous for its pretty fishing villages with picturesque names like Polperro, Mevagissey and Mousehole, as well as larger tourist resorts like Bude, St. Ives, Penzance, and Newlyn.

47 A Car maintenance

(J = Jane, R = Russell, S = Stranger)

(In a residential street – Russell is attending to his car)

J   Russell! What on earth are you doing?
R   Hold this for me, please.
J   Can't you get the car started?
R   Of course I can make it start. I'm just looking to see if everything is all right.
J   Didn't you have it serviced last week?
R   Yes. I'm just checking the engine, and the battery and the lights.

J	You had all those things checked at the garage.
R	But we're going away for the weekend.
J	And we must get everything ready. Now.
R	Exactly. You get all our things packed, and I'll check the car. I'll have it finished in a moment. Hey! Let me have the spanner.
J	Here you are!

Land's End – the first and last house in England

S	Hello, there! Can I help?
R	That's very kind of you. I think I can manage.
S	Don't let me stop you. You carry on with your work. I shan't say a word.
R	Oh – er – thanks.
S	What's the problem, then?
R	Oh, there isn't a problem. I'm just checking the engine . . .
S	Really! I've never seen it done like that before.
R	Well, it says here . . .
S	Oh, I see. A handbook. "How to make things work. How to get things done." Not much good, is it?
R	I don't know. I don't know much about cars.
S	I can see that. And I'm afraid books won't help you. They won't get your car running smoothly. Learn from experience. And from experts.
R	Like you.
S	Me? Oh, I'm not an expert. But perhaps I could help you. Now, listen . . . *(same scene, a little later)*
S	There are a lot of things wrong with this car. It needs servicing.
R	It went all right this morning.
S	Do you have it serviced properly?
R	Yes. Every six thousand miles. In fact, I had it serviced last week. And tested.
S	Tested?
R	Yes. I have it tested once a year. The MoT test.
S	Oh! The MoT test. But that's just to make the car safe to go on the road.
R	I get lots of things fixed at the same time – when I have the MoT test done.
S	Maybe. But you need to have your car thoroughly inspected. I've just looked at it.
R	Yes. I know you have.
S	You should have the engine tuned. And the clutch adjusted. And the sparking plugs replaced. And . . .
R	. . . the exhaust checked, perhaps?
S	Ah, the exhaust! You're quite right. The exhaust pipe is falling off. You see. You should get it fixed, shouldn't you? Or have a new one fitted.
R	Or have the car towed away.
S	Oh, no! You don't need to have the car towed away. We can fix the exhaust pipe now. You can fix it. No! You don't need the manual. Just do it yourself. *(later, the car is more or less in one piece)*
S	Can't you get it started?

R	No. It started all right this morning.
S	What are you doing now?
R	I'm letting the engine run. I'm getting it warmed up.
S	Yes. I can hear it. That's dangerous, you know.
R	Why?
S	The fumes. Can't you smell the fumes?
R	Er – yes. But they're not dangerous. We're in the open air.
S	That's right. The open air. Your car is poisoning the atmosphere.
R	No, it isn't.
S	Yes, it is, I'm afraid. All those fumes. All that smoke. The air's being poisoned. It's becoming polluted.
R	Polluted?
S	Yes. It's very unhealthy. It shouldn't be allowed. It should be made illegal.
R	I'll get it attended to.
J	What's happening? Russell, please stop the car making that dreadful noise. That's better. Look what you've done.
S	Let me help you.
J	That's very kind of you.
S	Don't mention it. I've been helping your husband to fix his car.
R	I didn't need any help.
J	I expect he did. He knows nothing about cars.
S	I think he needs a new car. I could sell him one. It's in excellent condition.
R	I'm sure it is.
S	I service it regularly. I keep the engine tuned. I . . .
R	It's very good of you, but I don't want to buy your car. I've got this one working now. And I'm going away for the weekend.

A cottage in Cornwall

	(later)
R	At last!
J	It's very late. We must go now. Oh, look. There's that charming man again.
R	Him! I wonder what he wants now.
J	Hello. What's wrong?
S	My car won't start.
R	Don't worry. The AA will be here in a few minutes. They'll get it started!

47

47 B Questions

In which part of Britain is Cornwall?
Why is the climate so mild there?
What holiday resorts are there?
What piece of advice did the stranger give to Russell?
How often does Russell have his car serviced?
Why is Russell's car poisoning the atmosphere?
What did the stranger want to sell Russell?

47 C And you?

Do you know a great deal about cars?
What things would you buy second-hand?

47 D have + object + past participle — lassen, veranlassen

have	object	past participle	
I'm having	the battery	changed.	*Ich lasse mir gerade die Batterie austauschen.*
I'll have	the car	washed.	*Ich werde das Auto waschen lassen.*
Do you have	it	tested regularly?	*Läßt du es regelmäßig überprüfen?*
I had	the engine	checked yesterday.	*Ich ließ gestern den Motor prüfen.*
I didn't have	the sparking plugs	renewed.	*Ich habe die Zündkerzen nicht erneuern lassen.*
Have	the clutch	adjusted.	*Lassen Sie die Kupplung einstellen.*
You need to have	your car	inspected.	*Sie müssen Ihr Auto durchsehen lassen.*
You ought to have	your watch	repaired.	*Sie sollten Ihre Uhr reparieren lassen.*

Wenn wir sagen wollen, daß wir etwas nicht selbst tun, sondern von jemand anderem machen lassen, verwenden wir die Konstruktion "have" + Objekt + Partizip Perfekt.
Unterscheiden Sie genau: I have the car tested. *Ich lasse das Auto testen.* I have tested the car. *Ich habe das Auto getestet.* In der Umgangssprache wird häufig "get" anstelle von "have" verwendet: I get a lot of things fixed at the same time.

47 E Translate the sentences:

Ich lasse mir gerade das Auto auftanken.
Ich habe es gesehen.
Sie ließen den Dieb verhaften.
Sie hat den Wasserhahn nicht
reparieren lassen.
Du mußt dein Visum (visa) für
Amerika erneuern lassen.
Ich lasse das Zimmer nächste
Woche ausmalen.
Ihr solltet diesen Baum nicht fällen lassen.
Sie hat den Anzug gereinigt.
Sie läßt den Anzug reinigen.
Laß dir die Haare schneiden.
Lassen Sie den Brief übersetzen.
Ich habe ihn schon übersetzt.

47 F make (have, let) + object + infinitive without "to" — veranlassen, zulassen

Old movies make me cry.
She makes her children
brush their teeth twice a day.
I won't let you disturb her.

Alte Filme bringen mich zum Weinen.
*Sie läßt ihre Kinder zweimal täglich
die Zähne putzen.*
*Ich werde nicht zulassen,
daß du sie störst.*

"Make" bzw. "have" + Objekt + Infinitiv ohne "to" verwenden wir im Sinne von *etwas veranlassen.* "Let" hingegen bedeutet *zulassen, gestatten, daß etwas gemacht wird.*

47 G Put in the English equivalent for the German „lassen, zulassen, veranlassen":

Yesterday he ... his car filled up at the garage.
I ... the car washed tomorrow.
Don't ... me stop you.
I don't think we should ... that car towed away.
You must ... the brakes adjusted.
He ... me laugh. (present tense)

47 H "do" and "make" machen, tun

> What have you done to that painting?
> He's made a hole in it.

Put in the correct form of "do" or "make":

Much progress ... in technology since World War II.
What are you ... the weekend after next?
He should have ... his homework.
She's always ... the same mistake.
Don't ... that noise!
I hate ... the cooking and washing-up.
Let's get somebody ... all the boring jobs.
She's just ... a cake.

47 I Fill in the correct preposition:

Don't stop. Carry ... with your work.
He doesn't know much ... politics.
I'm interested ... learning more about cars.
Let's get rid ... the bags.
We don't agree ... you there.
I couldn't find ... his telephone number.
She didn't believe ... his ability.
They argued ... the economic situation in Britain.

47 J Find the nouns to the following words and make sentences:

polluted – healthy – poisoned – dangerous – safe – expect – introduce – build – develop – describe

47 K A reservation letter

Book a room for 3 nights at the Mayflower Hotel, Plymouth.

47 L   Cornish 🆑

Cornish is a Celtic language, closely related to Breton and Welsh. Cornish was spoken in Cornwall until about a hundred and fifty years ago. Even today several thousand people learn and speak Cornish as a hobby; a few books and magazines are published in this language.

47 M   Situation – Say it in English

Sagen Sie, daß Sie sich entschlossen haben, Ihre nächsten Ferien in Cornwall zu verbringen.
Sagen Sie, daß Sie beabsichtigen, sich eine Halbtagsstellung zu suchen.
Ihr Gesprächspartner fragt Sie, was Sie veranlaßt hat, Ihre Meinung zu ändern.
Sagen Sie, daß Sie vorhaben, Betriebswirtschaft zu studieren.

47 N   Summary 🔊

Russell and Jane were going away for the weekend in their sports car. Russell had had the car serviced the previous week, but he just wanted to check if the engine, the battery, and the lights were all right. While he was doing this, a stranger came along and asked if he could help. He said he'd never seen an engine checked like that before, and was very amused to see that Russell was using a handbook – he said Russell should learn from experience and from experts, not from a book. He had a look at the car, and then told Russell that he should have the engine tuned, the clutch adjusted, the sparking plugs replaced, and the exhaust fixed. In fact Russell will *have* to get the exhaust fixed, as it fell off when the stranger kicked it! Eventually Russell did get the car started, whereupon the stranger said Russell shouldn't let the engine run so long, as it was polluting the air. When Jane came out with their luggage, Russell opened the car door and knocked her things all over the road. The kind stranger helped her pick them up. Then, when Jane and Russell were at last ready to set off on their holiday, they saw the stranger again – *his* car wouldn't start! Russell called to him that the AA (the Automobile Association) would soon be here to repair it, and off they went.

Every cloud has a silver lining

Vocabulary   **Wortschatz**

	English	IPA	German
47	southwesterly	saʊθˈwestəlɪ	südwestlich
	peninsula	pəˈnɪnsjʊlə	Halbinsel
	rocky	ˈrɒkɪ	felsig
	cliff	klɪf	Klippe, Felshang
	mild	maɪld	mild
	climate	ˈklaɪmət	Klima
	Gulf Stream	ˈgʌlf striːm	Golfstrom
	to warm	tə ˈwɔːm	(er)wärmen
	gentle	ˈdʒentl	sanft
	wooded	ˈwʊdɪd	bewaldet
	palm tree	ˈpɑːm triː	Palme
	tropical plant	trɒpɪkl ˈplɑːnt	tropische Pflanze
	tin	tɪn	Zinn
	mine	maɪn	Bergwerk, Grube, Zeche
	landscape	ˈlændskeɪp	Landschaft
	engine-house	ˈendʒən haʊs	Maschinenhalle
	china	ˈtʃaɪnə	Porzellan
	clay	kleɪ	Ton, Lehm
	pottery	ˈpɒtərɪ	Töpferei
	moon	muːn	Mond
	pyramid-shaped	ˈpɪrəmɪd ʃeɪpt	pyramidenförmig
	tip	tɪp	Halde
	tourism	ˈtʊərɪzm	Tourismus
	Knights of the Round Table	ˈnaɪts əv ðə ˈraʊnd ˈteɪbl	Ritter der Tafelrunde
	to give rise to	tə gɪv ˈraɪz tə	veranlassen, herbeiführen, bewirken
	romance	rəˈmæns	Romanze
	resort	rɪˈzɔːt	Ferienort
47 A	maintenance	ˈmeɪntənəns	Wartung, Instandhaltung
	to attend to	tʊ əˈtend tə	sich befassen mit, sich kümmern um
	to service	tə ˈsɜːvɪs	warten
	battery	ˈbætərɪ	Batterie
	to pack	tə ˈpæk	packen
	spanner	ˈspænə	Schraubenschlüssel
	handbook	ˈhændbʊk	Handbuch
	smoothly	ˈsmuːðlɪ	glatt, reibungslos
	MoT test (= Ministry of Transport vehicle test)	ˈem əʊ ˈtiː test (ˈmɪnɪstrɪ əv ˈtrɑːnspɔːt ˈvɪəkl test)	*(entspricht dem TÜV)*
	to fix	tə fɪks	in Ordnung bringen, reparieren, instandsetzen
	to inspect	tʊ ɪnˈspekt	prüfen

47

	to tune	tə ˈtjuːn	(Motor) einstellen
	to adjust	tʊ əˈdʒʌst	einstellen
	sparking plugs	ˈspɑːkɪŋ plʌgz	Zündkerzen
	exhaust	ɪgˈzɔːst	Auspuff
	exhaust pipe	ɪgˈzɔːst paɪp	Auspuffrohr
	to fall off	tə fɔːl ɒf	herunterfallen
	to tow away	tə ˈtəʊ əweɪ	abschleppen
	manual	ˈmænjʊəl	Handbuch
	fumes	fjuːmz	Abgase
	to smell	tə ˈsmel	riechen
	in the open air	ɪn ði ˈəʊpən ˈeə	im Freien
	to poison	tə ˈpɔɪzn	vergiften
	smoke	sməʊk	Rauch
	to pollute	tə pəˈluːt	verschmutzen
	unhealthy	ʌnˈhelθɪ	ungesund
	illegal	ɪˈliːgl	illegal, ungesetzlich
	the AA (= Automobile Association)	ði ˈeɪ ˈeɪ (ˈɔːtəməbiːl əsəʊsɪeɪʃn)	(der größte britische) Automobilklub
47 B	influence	ˈɪnflʊəns	Einfluß
47 D	to renew	tə rɪˈnjuː	erneuern
47 E	visa	ˈviːzə	Visum
47 G	brakes	breɪks	Bremsen
47 J	pollution	pəˈluːʃn	Verschmutzung
	poison	ˈpɔɪzn	Gift
	introduction	ɪntrəˈdʌkʃn	Einführung
47 L	Cornish	ˈkɔːnɪʃ	cornisch
	Breton	ˈbretn	bretonisch; Bretone, Bretonin
47 N	previous	ˈpriːvɪəs	vorhergehend
	amused	əˈmjuːzd	amüsiert, belustigt
	to kick	tə ˈkɪk	schlagen
	whereupon	ˈweərəpɒn	woraufhin
	Every cloud has a silver lining	evrɪ ˈklaʊd hæz ə sɪlvə ˈlaɪnɪŋ	Auf Regen folgt Sonnenschein

UNIT 48

Stonehenge

Stonehenge is one of the most famous prehistoric monuments in the world. The writer Henry James said "Stonehenge stands as lonely in history as it does on Salisbury Plain"; in all the world there is nothing quite like it. It took over three hundred years to build, from about 1,900 to about 1,600 B.C., and consists of a double circle of upright stones.

Outside the rings of stones is a circular bank with a ditch, about 320 feet across, and in the middle is a group of five huge stone arches called "trilithons".

Outside the bank to the northeast is a large stone called the "Heelstone". On Midsummer Day the sun rises directly over the Heelstone and shines into the centre of the circle, and on Midwinter Day the setting sun shines through the largest of the stone arches. What for? Why was Stonehenge built like this, nearly 4,000 years ago? For centuries, writers, historians and archaeologists have travelled to the desolate plain near Salisbury in Wiltshire to try to find out the answer to this question. They have put forward many theories: A sun temple? A computer for predicting the seasons and eclipses of the sun? But still the ancient stones have not given up all their secrets. Probably they never will.

48 A An accident

(PC S = Police Constable Smith, PC J = Police Constable Jones, W = Wife, C = Cyclist, D = Driver)

(The two policemen Smith and Jones walking down a quiet road)

PC S   Well, Jones, this is an important day in your life – your first day on the beat. What's wrong?
PC J   Er – being new to the job, I'm a bit nervous, actually.
PC S   You're not frightened of me, are you?
PC J   Oh, no! I'm glad to be on duty with an experienced officer like you.
PC S   Experienced and understanding. And alert.
PC J   Alert?
PC S   Doing a policeman's job, you must be alert at all times.
You must watch out for criminal activity.
PC J   Oh, I shall try to be alert. Really!
PC S   Of course, untrained recruits, like you, can't detect every crime committed.
But you can investigate anything happening that looks suspicious.
Jones, what are you doing?
PC J   I'm looking out for criminal activity. I'm trying to be alert.
PC S   You won't detect any crimes, staring into space. Ah ha! What was that?
PC J   That was breaking glass.
It sounded like an accident.
PC S   It might be a crime. You never know.
PC J   Good! Do you want me to investigate it?
PC S   Not on your own. We'll go together. United we stand!

(Further down the same street. A car has knocked down a female cyclist.)

W   Are you hurt?
C   No. I'm all right, thanks. Just a bit shaken.

Salisbury Cathedral, Wiltshire

D   You caused the accident, turning suddenly like that.
C   No. It was you, driving too close behind me.
D   Look at the lamp post – damaged beyond repair.
Look at my arm – probably broken.
Look at my car –
W   The car isn't badly damaged, and your arm isn't broken. Anyway, here are the police.
PC S   Oh dear, oh dear! Having a bit of trouble, I see.
D   Yes, officer. This young woman –
W   There's been an accident.
PC S   I can see that.
What are you doing now, Jones?
PC J   I'm taking down the registration number, checking to see if it's a stolen vehicle.
I'm calling –
PC S   I don't think that's necessary, Jones. Now, just help me for a moment.
I shall need statements from those of you directly involved in this incident, and from anyone witnessing it.
You, madam.

W	I was in the car, being driven by my husband here.
PC J	Do remember, madam, that anything you say will be taken down in writing and may be used in evidence against you.
PC S	Jones! You only say that when making an arrest. Sorry about that. It's his first day on duty.
D	Look at my car, officer. Aren't you going to inspect the damage?
PC S	That's a matter for your insurance company, sir. Your car is insured, I hope.
D	Of course.
PC S	You can make your statements at the police station. But we'll need a few details now. Jones! Where are you?
PC J	I'm here, taking measurements.
PC S	Well, you should be here with me, writing down details of the incident. You should not be there, standing in the road and causing an obstruction.
PC J	I was trying to be thorough and alert.

(driver and his wife filling out their insurance claim form at home)

D	I can't write with my wrist bandaged.
W	Let me do it, dear.
D	Oh, all right. Most of the form is filled in already.
W	Let's see. Name, address, car registration number, make of car, date and time of incident. Er – details of injuries sustained. I see there's a lot written down there about your wrist. But there's very little left to fill in.
D	What about the drawing of the accident?
W	Ah, yes. Here it is. Draw a plan in the space provided, indicating the position of all vehicles affected. Can't we get a plan from the police? The young constable was taking measurements in the road.
D	I wouldn't believe any measurements taken by that young idiot. Anyway, we have to give our version of the accident. It's certain to be different from the one drawn up by the police.
W	And it's certain to be different from the one given by the girl on the bicycle.

(PC Smith taking a statement from the cyclist)

PC S	What was the approximate time of the incident?
C	Eleven thirty. You know that. You were in the same street.
PC S	Yes, madam. But I need your version of what happened. What were you doing at the time stated?
C	I was cycling home. This car ran into me from behind when I stopped.
PC S	What caused you to stop?
C	A dog running into the road.
PC S	Excuse me, madam. I need another pen. I'll get one from Constable Jones. Where is he?
C	Just behind you.
PC S	What have you been doing? Where have you been?
PC J	I went to the scene of the incident involving you and the motor car, madam.
PC S	And then?
PC J	I was struck by a passing car.
PC S	Not looking where you were going, I suppose?
PC J	No. Just trying to be alert. I think I'm learning.

48

48 B Questions

In which county is Stonehenge?
When was it probably constructed?
Why is the young constable so nervous?
Who do you think caused the accident?
Why did the cyclist stop?

48 C And you?

Have you ever been involved in or witnessed an accident?
Give a short report of what you saw or did.

48 D Participles   Partizipien

I'm **trying** to be alert.	*Ich versuche, wachsam zu sein.*
I've **forgotten** your name.	*Ich habe Ihren Namen vergessen.*
His name will never be **forgotten**.	*Sein Name wird nie vergessen werden.*

"Trying" ist ein "present participle" (Partizip Präsens, Mittelwort der Gegenwart); "forgotten" ist ein "past participle" (Partizip Perfekt, Mittelwort der Vergangenheit). "To be + present participle" ist die Verlaufsform (I'm trying). "To have + past participle" ist das Perfekt (I've forgotten), während "to be + past participle" die Formen des Passivs ergibt (will be forgotten). Beide Partizipien kommen auch als gewöhnliche Adjektive vor (an interesting story, a stolen car).

48 E Participle clauses (I)   Partizipialsätze

a) Partizipien anstelle von Nebensätzen des Grundes

Being new to the job, I'm a bit nervous. (= Because / As / Since I'm new to the job . . .)	*Da ich in dem Beruf neu bin, bin ich etwas nervös.*
Not knowing what to do, he asked a policeman for help. (= Because / As / Since he didn't know . . .)	*Da er nicht wußte, was er tun sollte, bat er einen Polizisten um Hilfe.*

Beachten Sie: Bei der Verkürzung von kausalen Nebensätzen fällt die Konjunktion (as, since, because) immer weg.

b) Partizipien anstelle von Nebensätzen der Zeit

Seeing the accident, the young constable fainted.	*Als er den Unfall sah, wurde der junge Polizist ohnmächtig.*
You only say that when making an arrest.	*Man sagt das nur, wenn man jemanden verhaftet.*
Having written the letter, she posted it. (= After having written . . .) (= After writing . . .)	*Nachdem sie den Brief geschrieben hatte, gab sie ihn zur Post.*

Bei der Verkürzung temporaler Nebensätze bleibt die Konjunktion (when, while, after, before) oft zur Verdeutlichung erhalten.

c) Partizipien anstelle von Relativsätzen

What caused you to stop?	*Was hat Sie veranlaßt zu halten?*
A dog running into the road.	*Ein Hund, der in die Straße lief.*
It was a car offered for sale in the newspaper.	*Es war ein Auto, das in der Zeitung zum Verkauf angeboten wurde.*

d) Partizipien zur Verbindung zweier oder mehrerer Hauptsätze

I'm here, taking measurements.	*Ich bin hier und messe ab.*
Well, you should be here with me, writing down details of the incident.	*Nun, Sie sollten hier bei mir sein und Einzelheiten des Vorfalls aufschreiben.*

In allen Beispielsätzen handelt es sich um die verbundene Partizipialkonstruktion, d. h. wir haben dasselbe Subjekt für den Hauptsatz und die Partizipialkonstruktion. Dabei besteht zwischen dem Partizip Präsens und dem konjugierten Verb des Hauptsatzes in der Regel Gleichzeitigkeit (z. B. Being new to the job, I'm a bit nervous. Aber: After writing the letter, she posted it.), während das Partizip Perfekt stets Vorzeitigkeit gegenüber der Handlung des Hauptsatzes ausdrückt (Having written the letter, she posted it.).
Die Art der Beziehung des Partizips zum Hauptsatz (Zeit, Grund, Relativsatz) muß aus dem Zusammenhang erschlossen werden.
Die mit dem "ing"- bzw. "ed"-Partizip verkürzten Nebensätze gehören vorwiegend der Schriftsprache an. In Prüfungen wird meist die Auflösung der Partizipialkonstruktion in einen solchen Nebensatz oder die Übertragung ins Deutsche verlangt, gelegentlich auch die Bildung einer Partizipialkonstruktion (vgl. auch Unit 50).

48 F   Give the German equivalent of the following sentences:

Being very rich, Mr Trump can afford a yacht.
Having won the football pools, Jane bought a house in the South of France.
Not being able to change the wheel, she asked another driver to give her a lift.
Having finished the article, I had a cup of tea.
She never buys the products advertised on television.
The language spoken in Brazil is Portuguese.
I heard a concert given by the New York Philharmonic Orchestra.
The young girl injured in the accident was taken to hospital.

Now rewrite the sentences, replacing the participial construction with a sub-clause.

48 G Change the sentences, using the participle:

When I heard the news, I went home.
The policeman who asked her about the accident was very polite.
Since they lived in the country, they had few visits from their friends.
While I was walking in the park, I met Jane.
After she had filled in the insurance form, she sent it to the insurance company straight away.
You should be careful when you drive beside a cyclist.
He sat in the armchair and smoked a pipe.
When you telephone someone in London from abroad, just dial 1, not 01.

48 H Use a participle clause to translate the sentences:

Du mußt aufpassen, wenn du die Straße überquerst.
Das Auto, das man mir gestern angeboten hat, war bereits verkauft.
Wer war der Mann, der in dem Pub mit Ihnen gesprochen hat?
Da er sehr müde war, ging er früh schlafen.
Da er sich krank fühlte, wollte er seine Rede nicht halten.
Da er nicht Französisch konnte, konnte er sich nicht verständlich machen.
Die Leute, die in den Unfall verwickelt waren, haben ihre Aussagen gemacht.
Der Zahnarzt, der mir von einem Freund empfohlen wurde, ist sehr gut.

48 I Pronunciation

Find the word with the same sound:

cr**i**me	a) wr**i**st	b) dr**i**ve	c) **i**f
inc**i**dent	a) l**i**ke	b) s**i**r	c) **i**nto
y**ou**ng	a) br**ou**ght	b) s**ou**nd	c) h**u**ngry
gl**a**d	a) l**a**nguage	b) m**a**ke	c) f**a**r
br**ea**king	a) s**ea**	b) w**ai**t	c) br**ea**kfast
d**ow**n	a) n**ou**n	b) **ow**n	c) l**ow**
d**e**tails	a) to b**e**t	b) to r**ea**d	c) r**ea**dy
v**er**sion	a) to **ear**n	b) t**e**rrace	c) h**ere**

48 J Explain these words

experienced – investigate – detect – vehicle – on duty – different

48 K An insurance form

48 L Situation – Say it in English

Ein Kollege hatte vor einiger Zeit einen Unfall.
Sagen Sie, daß es Ihnen leid tut, davon zu hören.
Bieten Sie Ihrem Kollegen Ihre Hilfe an.
Wünschen Sie ihm gute Besserung.
Sagen Sie ihm, daß Sie sich freuen, ihn nächste Woche wiederzusehen.
Sagen Sie ihm, daß er sich keine Sorgen zu machen braucht über seine Stellung, daß alles in Ordnung kommen wird.
Raten Sie ihm, daß Sie an seiner Stelle nicht zu früh wieder ins Büro kommen würden.
Empfehlen Sie ihm, längere Zeit Ferien zu machen.

48 M Summary

It was Police Constable Jones's first day on the beat. PC Smith, an older, more experienced officer, accompanied him and reminded him that it was very important to be alert when looking out for criminal activity. PC Smith was interrupted by a tremendous crash – a car had hit a girl riding a bicycle. PC Smith, accompanied by PC Jones, walked over to the scene of the accident. The driver of the car said the girl had caused the accident by turning suddenly, but the girl said it was the car driver's fault.

PC Jones began taking down the car's registration number, checking to see if it was a stolen vehicle, but PC Smith said he needn't do that. At home, the car driver and his wife filled in a form for their insurance company, while at the police station PC Smith took a statement from the girl cyclist. In the middle of this, PC Jones arrived back with his clothes all torn. While taking measurements at the scene of the accident, he'd been struck by a passing car.

All beginnings are hard

Vocabulary / Wortschatz

48	B.C. (= before Christ)	ˈbiː ˈsiː (bɪˈfɔː ˈkraɪst)	vor Christus
	circle	ˈsɜːkl	Kreis, Ring
	stone	stəʊn	Stein(block)
	circular	ˈsɜːkjʊlə	kreisförmig, rund
	bank	bæŋk	*hier:* Erdwall
	ditch	dɪtʃ	Graben
	arch	ɑːtʃ	Bogen
	trilithon	ˈtraɪlɪθɒn	Bogen aus drei behauenen Steinen
	Midsummer Day	ˈmɪdsʌmə ˈdeɪ	Sommersonnenwende
	to shine, shone, shone	tə ˈʃaɪn, ʃɒn, ʃɒn	scheinen, leuchten
	Midwinter Day	ˈmɪdwɪntə ˈdeɪ	Wintersonnenwende
	the setting sun	ðə ˈsetɪŋ ˈsʌn	die untergehende Sonne
	historian	hɪˈstɔːrɪən	Historiker(in)
	archaeologist	ɑːkɪˈɒlədʒɪst	Archäologe, Archäologin
	desolate	ˈdesələt	verlassen, einsam
	plain	pleɪn	Ebene
	to put forward a theory	tə ˈpʊt fɔːwəd ə ˈθɪərɪ	eine Theorie aufstellen
	sun temple	ˈsʌn templ	Sonnentempel
	to predict	tə prɪˈdɪkt	vorhersagen, voraussagen, prophezeien
	eclipse of the sun	ɪˈklɪps əv ðə ˈsʌn	Sonnenfinsternis
48 A	constable	ˈkʌnstəbl	Schutzmann, Polizist
	cyclist	ˈsaɪklɪst	Radfahrer(in)
	on the beat	ˈɒn ðə ˈbiːt	auf Streife, auf Rundgang, auf Tour
	to be frightened of s.b.	tə bɪ ˈfraɪtnd əv	Angst haben vor jdm.

	on duty	ɒn ˈdjuːtɪ	im Dienst
	experienced	ɪkˈspɪərɪənst	erfahren
	understanding	ʌndəˈstændɪŋ	verständnisvoll
	alert	əˈlɜːt	wachsam
	untrained recruits	ˌʌntreɪnd rɪˈkruːts	ungeschulte, nicht eingearbeitete Rekruten
	to detect	tə dɪˈtekt	aufdecken, entdecken
	suspicious	səˈspɪʃəs	verdächtig, mißtrauisch
	to stare into space	tə ˈsteər ɪntə ˈspeɪs	in die Luft starren
	further down	ˈfɜːðə ˈdaʊn	weiter unten
	to knock down	tə ˈnɒk ˈdaʊn	umfahren
	shaken	ˈʃeɪkən	durcheinander, mitgenommen
	close	kləʊs	nahe
	lamp post	ˈlæmp pəʊst	Laternenpfahl
	beyond repair	bɪˈjɒnd rɪˈpeə	irreparabel
	to take down	tə teɪk ˈdaʊn	notieren
	car registration number	ˈkɑː redʒɪˈstreɪʃn nʌmbə	Autokennzeichen
	statement	ˈsteɪtmənt	Aussage
	incident	ˈɪnsɪdənt	Zwischenfall
	to witness	tə ˈwɪtnəs	Zeuge sein
	to take down in writing	tə ˈteɪk daʊn ɪn ˈraɪtɪŋ	schriftlich niederlegen
	to make an arrest	tə ˈmeɪk ən əˈrest	verhaften
	insured	ɪnˈʃʊəd, ɪnˈʃɔːd	versichert
	obstruction	əbˈstrʌkʃn	Hindernis
	claim	kleɪm	Anspruch, Forderung
	wrist	rɪst	Handgelenk
	bandaged	ˈbændɪdʒd	eingebunden
	make of car	ˈmeɪk əv ˈkɑː	Automarke
	injury	ˈɪndʒərɪ	Verletzung
	to sustain	tə səˈsteɪn	erleiden
	to draw	tə ˈdrɔː	zeichnen
	to indicate	tʊ ˈɪndɪkeɪt	angeben, anzeigen, markieren
	approximate	əˈprɒksɪmət	annähernd
	at the time stated	ət ðə ˈtaɪm ˈsteɪtɪd	zur angegebenen Zeit
	to cycle	tə ˈsaɪkl	radfahren
	to strike, struck, struck	tə ˈstraɪk, strʌk, strʌk	stoßen, schlagen
48 B	to construct	tə kənˈstrʌkt	errichten
48 E	to faint	tə ˈfeɪnt	ohnmächtig werden
48 F	yacht	jɒt	Yacht
	injured	ˈɪndʒəd	verletzt
48 G	beside	bɪˈsaɪd	neben, dicht bei
48 M	to accompany	tʊ əˈkʌmpənɪ	begleiten
	crash	kræʃ	Krach, Aufprall
	to ride a bicycle	tə ˈraɪd ə ˈbaɪsɪkl	auf einem Rad fahren

48

UNIT 49

A pub isn't just a drinking place. For many English people, the pub on the corner is the centre of their social life. It's a kind of club where friends – and strangers – can come together to talk about business, sport, the weather, or anything they like, over a drink.

Confusion often arises because of the licensing hours. The stringent licensing laws with the 11 o'clock closing time were introduced during World War I to stop drunkenness among munition workers. Relaxed laws came into force in November 2005. They allow pubs, bars and clubs to apply for longer opening hours. Most pubs have a dartboard and a pub darts team, and darts is now so popular that it is regularly shown on television. There are many different games you can play with a dartboard and some darts. The commonest game is "301", in which each player starts with 301 points and the points he scores with his darts are subtracted from that number until he reaches nought.

49 A The Darts Champion

(F = Fred, R = Russell, B = Bill, S = Stan, J = Jane)

(An English Pub)

F   Double twenty again.
You're in good form tonight, Russell.

R   Not bad, eh?
I'm always in good form before a match even if it's only a friendly match.

F   If you play like that tonight, we'll win very easily.

R   Whose turn is it now?

B   It's my turn to throw and your turn to buy a round.

R   Is it? What, again?

R	Okay. What'll you have?
B	Same again, please. A pint of bitter.
F	I think I'll have a half of brown.
R	Two pints of bitter and a half of brown, please.
S	That'll be one pound fifty.

(Russell pays, comes back with drinks and bumps into Bill)

R	I'm terribly sorry.
B	That's all right.
R	Here you are.
B	Cheers!
F	Cheers! Let's put the drinks over there so we don't knock them over.
R	How are you getting on?
F	Bill's in good form today. He's just scored two fifties.
B	That's extremely difficult. Have you ever seen anyone do that before?
R	Oh yes, of course I have. But I've never seen you do that before.
B	It's your throw now.

R	Three triple twenties. Have you ever seen that before?
B	Oh well. It's fairly easy if you have your foot over the line.
R	Oh, did I?
B	They put the line there in order to make it more difficult to throw triple twenties.
R	Have you ever seen that before?
B	Shall we get a bigger dartboard, Fred?
F	Ha, ha. Where on earth are the Royal Oak team? They're awfully late. It's after nine already.
R	Well, if they don't come by 9.30, they've lost.
B	Oh come on, Russell, it's only a friendly match. It doesn't matter if they're a bit late.
F	A bit late! They're dreadfully late!
B	They've got a long way to come.
F	Well, if they know they've got a long way to come, they should leave earlier so as to get here on time.
S	I hope they do come though. I want to see the Midlands champion play. He's in their team, isn't he?
R	Yes, that's right.
S	Have you ever seen him play?
R	No, I've never seen him play.
F	Neither have I. But they say he's pretty good.
B	He comes from London, doesn't he?
S	And now he plays for the Royal Oak team. They haven't lost a match since he came.
R	We'll see about that.
F	We'd better have another drink. Same again, please, Stan.
R	Look, it's ten o'clock already. It's getting rather late.
J	Hello.
B	Hello.
F	Hello.
R	Good evening.
J	Are you the darts team?

R	That's right.
	What can we do for you?
J	I'm Jane Egan.
	I'm from the Royal Oak.
	I'm terribly sorry I'm late.
	There was a long traffic jam on the motorway.
F	Where are the others?
J	The team captain asked me to apologise for him but he's in bed with flu and three other members of the team are ill, too.
	So I'm the only one who can come.
B	Okay. Let's have a quick game then.
R	I don't think I've ever played against a woman before.
F	But wait a minute.
	There are three of us and there's only one of them.
	What do the rules say about that?
R	I don't know.
B	I don't know either.
	What do you think, Stan?
S	Just a moment.
	I'll have a look in the rule book.
	"… In order to decide who shall begin, each player shall throw one dart …"
	No, wait a minute.
	"… Each player shall remove his own darts from the board in order to avoid accidents …"
	Hm, there's nothing about a different number of players in the teams.
	I'd suggest you three throw one dart each, and the lady throws three darts.
R	That's a very good idea. All right.
	Here are the darts.
R	One for you, one for you.
J	I've got my own darts.
R	You throw first, you're the guest.
J	No, I'd much rather you went first.
	I'll get my darts while you start.
S	Time gentlemen. Last orders please!
R	Twenty. That's pretty good for a start.
B	Well, it's fairly good.
	Oh well, it was nearly a twenty.
R	That makes twenty-one.
F	Double fifteen.
R	So the Long Hall have scored fifty-one.
	Fifty-one from three hundred and one makes two hundred and fifty.
	Now it's your turn.

R	Well done.
F	Fantastic!
B	Hm, beginner's luck.
R	Hey!
F	Not bad.
B	A hundred and twenty.
R	A hundred and eighty.
	You play like a champion.
J	Actually I am the champion.
	I'm the Midlands champion.

49 B Questions

Is darts of British or American origin?
Where is the Midlands champion from?
Why can't the captain of the "Royal Oak" team come?
How many darts does each player usually have?
How did they solve the problem of the different number of players in the teams?

49 C And you?

What do you think about the licensing hours in British pubs? Give your opinion in two or three sentences.
Compare the British pub with a similar institution in your country.
Can you explain how darts is played?

49 D Adverbs of degree   **Gradadverbien**

That's **extremely** difficult.	*Das ist äußerst schwierig.*
They're **awfully** late.	*Sie sind furchtbar spät dran.*
I'm **terribly** sorry.	*Es tut mir schrecklich leid.*
That's a **very** good idea.	*Das ist eine sehr gute Idee.*

Adverbien, die einen gewissen Grad hinsichtlich der Intensität ausdrücken, mit der das jeweilige Bezugswort (Adverb, Adjektiv oder Verb) beschrieben wird, bezeichnet man als Gradadverbien, z. B.: very difficult, *sehr schwierig,* extremely difficult, *äußerst schwierig.* Zur Adverbbildung vgl. Band 2, Unit 26.

Achten Sie auf den wichtigen Unterschied zwischen Adjektiv und Adverb:

> Jane looked beautiful in her red dress.
> Russell walked slowly through Central Park.

Im ersten Satz bezieht sich *beautiful* auf das Substantiv *Jane.* Im zweiten Satz dagegen bezieht sich *slowly* auf das Verb *walked.*

49 E Put the correct form of the adjective or adverb into these sentences:

We saw a very … play at the theatre. (good)
John played football very … last Saturday. (good)
The film we saw last night was … boring. (terrible)
The photographs are … nice. (extreme)
He's a … driver. (dangerous)
He always drives too … (fast)
The coffee tasted … (awful)
I'm … sorry I'm late. (awful)
He looked around … (careful)
The young woman looked … in her red dress. (beautiful)
He … offered us another room. (quick)
She was … disappointed. (deep)
They ought to play … (fair)
We must train … for the next match. (hard)

49 F very / very much   sehr

It was a very exciting match.
She played very well.
I enjoyed it very much.

"Very" steht bei Adjektiven und Adverbien, "very much" steht bei Verben.

Use the correct form of the German „sehr":

The players are in … good form.   Thank you …
We liked the evening …   I'm … sorry indeed.
They were … surprised to see Jane win.   I regret … what happened.

49 G fairly / rather / pretty / quite   ziemlich

Häufig entsprechen alle vier Adverbien dem deutschen *ziemlich*. "Quite" hat die zusätzliche Bedeutung von *ganz, völlig* (It's quite impossible.).
"Fairly" und "rather" haben oft eine subjektive, wertende Färbung.

It's fairly warm.   *(es gefällt mir so)*
It's rather cold.   *(es ist nicht angenehm so)*

Die Verbindung "rather" + positives Adjektiv (good, well, nice, pleasant) hat die Bedeutung "very", "extremely":

Your English is rather good.   *sehr gut*
It was rather a nice evening.   *ein sehr netter Abend*

49 H Put in "fairly" or "rather":

This exercise is not too bad. It's … easy.
I'm … tired. Let's go.
Your car is … slow. You should get a new one.
I want a larger car. But they're … expensive.
He plays the trumpet … well, but he still needs a lot of practice.
You play … well. Please come and play again.

49 I too / also / as well   auch

Three other members of the team are ill, too.
I like playing tennis. I do, too.
I don't enjoy watching cricket. I don't either.

"Too" steht gewöhnlich am Satzende. Gleichbedeutend mit "too" ist "as well": They're ill as well. Man kann auch "also" verwenden, das seltener am Satzende steht: They're also ill.
In verneinten Sätzen steht anstelle von "too", "also" und "as well" immer "not either".

Translate the sentences:

Haben Sie auch *David Copperfield* gelesen?
Sie hat auch zwei Hunde und eine Katze.
Ich kann morgen auch nicht kommen.

Du mußt die Zündkerzen auch auswechseln.
Meine Cousine kann auch nicht schwimmen.

49 J Clauses of purpose — Absichtssätze

They put the line there **in order to** make it more difficult to throw triple twenties.
Let's put the drinks over there **so** we don't knock them over.
If they know they've got a long way to come, they should leave earlier **so as to** get here on time.

Absicht oder Zweck kann man durch "to", "in order to", "so as to" ausdrücken. Man kann auch einen Nebensatz bilden, eingeleitet durch "so that", "so" *so daß, damit*.

49 K Form one sentence, replacing "to want to" with the word or words in brackets:

I watch the programme. I want to learn English. (to)
He goes to the pub. He wants to play darts. (so that)
We left early. We wanted to get there on time. (so as to)
Let's train hard. We want to win next time. (so that)
She drove slowly. She wanted to avoid an accident. (in order to)

49 L ever — je, jemals

Have you ever seen him play?
No, I've never seen him play.

Hast du ihn je(mals) spielen sehen?
Nein, ich habe ihn niemals (noch nie) spielen sehen.

Verbindungen mit "ever"

Whoever rings, tell him I'm very busy.
Wer auch immer anruft, sage ihm, ich sei sehr beschäftigt.

Wherever you go, I'll go with you.
Wo auch immer du hingehst, ich werde mit dir gehen.

Whatever you say to her, she keeps smiling.
Was auch immer Sie zu ihr sagen, sie lächelt.

Come and see me **whenever** you're in London.
Besuche mich, wann immer du in London bist.

Die Verbindungen mit "ever" stehen in der Bedeutung "it doesn't matter who, what, when, where" und verbinden zwei Sätze miteinander, z. B. It doesn't matter where you go. I'll go with you. = Wherever you go, I'll go with you.

49 M Translate the sentences:

Bist du schon einmal in New York gewesen?
Wo immer wir hinkamen, wir fanden die Leute sehr freundlich.
Wann auch immer er nach Paris kam, er wohnte immer im Plaza Hotel.
Wer immer Sie sind, ich bin nicht interessiert.
Welche Probleme Sie auch haben, Sie können immer zu mir kommen.

49 N Pronunciation

Underline the stressed syllable of the following words:

champion – tonight – terribly – difficult – traffic jam – motorway – different – beginner – actually – accident – suggest – minute

49 O Vocabulary

Give the opposite of the following adjectives:

difficult – big – late – long – right – better – quick – a different number of players

49 P Situation – Say it in English

Sie sind in einem englischen Pub.
Der Wirt fragt Sie, was Sie haben möchten.
Sagen Sie, daß Sie ein kleines Bier (half a pint of bitter) haben möchten.
Ihr Gesprächspartner hat sich verspätet. Wie entschuldigt er sich?
Wie reagieren Sie?
Schlagen Sie Ihrem Freund vor, die Gläser woanders hinzustellen, damit Sie sie nicht umstoßen.
Sagen Sie, daß es ziemlich spät wird.
Sagen Sie, daß Sie hoffen, daß Frank doch kommt.
Schlagen Sie Ihrem Gesprächspartner vor, nicht mehr länger zu warten.
Sagen Sie, daß es Ihnen Spaß gemacht hat, mit ihm zu reden.

49 Q Summary

It was the night of a friendly darts match between two pubs, the "Long Hall" and the "Royal Oak". The members of the "Long Hall" team were waiting in the bar of their pub for the "Royal Oak" team to arrive. While they waited, they played darts, of course. Russell was in good form, and threw several double twenties, but Bill was in even better form – he threw two fifties. Bill asked Russell if he'd ever seen anyone do that before; Russell said he had, but he'd never seen Bill do that before. In fact Russell was in extremely good form – he threw three triple twenties, the highest possible score. Poor Fred was in rather bad form and couldn't even hit the dartboard. It began to get late, and still the "Royal Oak" team hadn't arrived. Stan, the barkeeper, said he very much wanted to see the Midlands champion play, who was a member of the "Royal Oak" team. At last, at ten o'clock Jane arrived and apologised for the other members of the "Royal Oak" team – she was the only one who had been able to come. They decided to play a game of darts, though Russell said he didn't think he'd ever played against a woman before. Stan suggested each member of the "Long Hall" team should throw one dart and Jane should throw three darts. With their three darts, the "Long Hall" scored 51. Then Jane threw her darts – and scored three triple twenties! She was the Midlands champion!

One for the road

Vocabulary — Wortschatz

49	social	ˈsəʊʃl	Gesellschafts-, gesellschaftlich
	club	klʌb	Klub, Verein
	confusion	kənˈfjuːʒn	Verwirrung
	licensing hours	ˈlaɪsənsɪŋ aʊəz	Lizenz-, Schankstunden
	licensing laws	ˈlaɪsənsɪŋ lɔːz	Lizenz-, Konzessionsgesetze
	standard	ˈstændəd	normal, vorschriftsmäßig
	dartboard	ˈdɑːtbɔːd	Zielscheibe

	darts	dɑːts		Spicker, Pfeile; Pfeilwerfen
	to score points	tə ˈskɔː ˈpɔɪnts		Punkte erzielen
	to subtract	tə səbˈtrækt		abziehen
49 A	champion	ˈtʃæmpjən		Meister(in)
	to be in good form	tə bɪ ɪn ˈgʊd ˈfɔːm		gut in Form sein
	to throw	tə ˈθrəʊ		werfen
	to knock over	tə ˈnɒk ˈəʊvə		umwerfen, umstoßen
	fairly	ˈfeəlɪ		ziemlich
	triple	ˈtrɪpl		dreifach
	team captain	ˈtiːm ˈkæptən		Mannschaftskapitän, -führer
	rules	ruːlz		Spielregeln
	in order to	ɪn ˈɔːdə tə		um zu
	to remove	tə rɪˈmuːv		wegnehmen, forträumen, beseitigen
	it's your turn	ɪts ˈjɔː tɜːn		Sie sind an der Reihe, du bist an der Reihe
49 B	origin	ˈɒrɪdʒɪn		Ursprung
49 F	surprised	səˈpraɪzd		überrascht
49 L	whoever	huːˈevə		wer (auch) immer
	whatever	wɒtˈevə		was (auch) immer
	whenever	wenˈevə		wann (auch) immer
49 Q	score	skɔː		Punktezahl
	the highest possible score	ðə ˈhaɪɪst ˈpɒsəbl ˈskɔː		die höchstmögliche Punktezahl
	barkeeper	ˈbɑːkiːpə		Schankwirt, Kneipenwirt
	one for the road	ˈwʌn fə ðə ˈrəʊd		*(ehe der Gast sich verabschiedet, bietet man ihm ein Glas auf [für] den Weg an)*

UNIT 50

(CB) Breakfast television has been an institution in America for many years, but it only reached Britain in 1982, when both the British television networks, the BBC (British Broadcasting Corporation) and the IBA (Independent Broadcasting Authority) started breakfast shows. These programmes, shown from about 6 in the morning to about 10, rapidly became popular.

The arrival of breakfast-time television was, however, only part of a revolution in the media in the early 1980's caused by great advances in communications technology. Cable television, financed by a sponsorship system, in which sponsors buy broadcasting time from the cable companies and show their own programmes, has greatly increased the possible number of channels. The BBC, being a public corporation, gets all its money from radio and television licences, and shows no advertising at all. The IBA is financed through advertising – advertisers buy advertising time in which to show commercials.

50 A Breakfast Television

(P = Presenter, PR = Producer, C = Cleaner, CC = Cookery Correspondent, RC = Racing Correspondent, W = Weather man, A = Arnold, R = Reporter)

P   Hello. This is "Breakfast Time", your favourite early morning show, coming to you from the studios of Windsor Television.
Actually it isn't. I'm just getting ready for the show. It's your chance to see one of your favourite TV personalities preparing to bring you an hour of news and comment from around the world.

P	As you can see, we're pretty busy.
PR	Er – Jim!
P	Excuse me. Listen! You know I don't like to be interrupted while rehearsing my show. Sorry! That was the producer of the show. I expect she'll be here in a moment.
PR	Hey, Jim! What are you doing?
P	Rehearsing my show while waiting for my breakfast.
PR	Breakfast! Breakfast is for your viewers, not for you. And we're on the air in a few minutes.
P	People watching my show want to see a happy, well-fed Jim Cool.
PR	If we don't improve the show soon, there won't be any people watching it.
P	It's an excellent show. What do you think of it?
C	Well, I sometimes hear people talking about it – asking each other what it's like.
P	Why do they do that?
C	Well, not many of them actually watch it.
P	All right. Will you get my breakfast while I discuss the show with the producer?
PR	Right, Jim. Let's look at today's headlines. What are the main news stories?
P	Well, after looking at the morning papers, I've realised that there isn't much news today.
PR	No disasters? No wars? Nothing happening to the Royal Family?
P	I'm afraid not.
PR	Let's see what our correspondents have to report then.
P	And waiting for us is our industrial correspondent in the Midlands.
P	Good morning, Frank. Any news of the strike?

(Frank appears, but he can't be heard because of the noise)

P	That noise means the strike is over. So there's no story there.
PR	Who's next?
CC	You'll have to cancel the cookery lesson this morning, Jim. I've just destroyed the kitchen, trying out my new gas cooker.
P	Oh, no! What about sport?
RC	I'm on the course at Kempton Park, Jim, waiting for the fog to clear. But I expect today's meeting will be cancelled.
P	And I had money on the favourite!
PR	Don't waste time, Jim. We need news. And we need it fast.
P	Well, there's always the weather. Let's see what the forecast is for today.
W	The satellite pictures just coming in show a deep depression approaching from the Atlantic. This, combined with strong winds from the South West –
P	I'm afraid your picture's gone.
W	Thank you. Oh dear! I must have my satellite picture. Where's it gone? Where's the weather? It was there a moment ago.
P	Don't go! Get him back! You're the producer!
PR	Ah, but it's *your* show, Jim. You always say that when the viewing figures are good. Anyway, who's next?
P	It's Arnold, the fitness expert.
A	Sorry, Jim. I can't do anything for you this morning. I broke this when practising a new exercise. You can use the film of me showing people how to –

P	Thank you, Arnold. I think that's enough.
PR	Is there any news from our roving reporter?
P	He's been in Wales, filming a schoolmaster climbing a mountain.
PR	That doesn't sound very exciting.
P	Well, our reporter thinks it is. Let's have a look at the film.
R	This is your roving reporter, bringing you the latest news of Trevor Jones, the Welsh schoolmaster pushing that pea up to the top of Snowdon, the highest mountain in Wales. He is now in his third day on the mountain. Now, Trevor – I hope you don't mind me calling you Trevor – how do you feel leaving your family, spending three nights on the mountain just in order to push that pea up to the top of Snowdon? Trevor – er, should I call you Trev? Er – Trev – er – Mr Jones – I think he only speaks Welsh. Listen, Trevor. You speak to us in Welsh, if you like, and we'll add sub-titles in English, for our viewers in England.
PR	No. We shan't have sub-titles in any language. And we shan't have that film. Now, what about the interview on the economic situation?
P	Cancelled, I'm afraid.
C	There are always the commercials, you know.
PR	Our viewers don't just want to see commercials while eating breakfast.
P	Breakfast! Where's my breakfast?
C	It'll be coming in a moment.
P	I've got it!
PR	Your breakfast?
P	No, I've got an idea.
PR	Well, hurry up! We're going on the air soon.

(a few minutes later)

P	Good morning. This is your favourite breakfast television show, coming to you from the studios of Windsor Television, situated on the banks of the River Thames. And today we have a special edition of the programme for you. You will actually be able to see your own presenter, Jim Cool – that's me – actually eating his own breakfast. So, what's special on the menu today?

50 B Questions

What sort of programme is "Breakfast Time"?
What is the presenter doing at the beginning of the story?
What is the presenter expecting from the industrial correspondent?
Why is the presenter of the show not happy about the fact that the meeting at Kempton Park has been cancelled?
What was the presenter doing when the programme went on the air?

50 C   And you?

Do you watch a lot of television?
What sort of programmes do you like best?
What advantage has television over radio?

50 D   Participle clauses (II)   Partizipialsätze

a)

> This is your favourite breakfast television show, coming to you from the studios of Windsor Television, situated on the banks of the River Thames.

Die ing-Form "coming" steht hier satzverkürzend für einen Relativsatz (which is coming), ebenso das nachgestellte Perfektpartizip "situated" (which are situated).

b)

> The weather being fine, we went for a walk.
> The headlines having been checked, Jim continued his breakfast.
> The cookery lesson being cancelled, something else has to be found.

In diesen Beispielsätzen hat die Partizipialkonstruktion ein eigenes Subjekt, es handelt sich um ein unverbundenes oder absolutes Partizip. Häufig steht "with" am Anfang eines solchen absoluten Partizipialsatzes: With the cookery lesson being cancelled, something else has to be found. *Da die Kochstunde gestrichen ist, muß etwas anderes gefunden werden.*

50 E   Shorten the following sentences if possible:

After he had studied at Berkeley, he became a lawyer.
Will you get my breakfast while I discuss the show with the producer?
You should fasten your seat bealts when you're driving.
Because I didn't know what to do, I telephoned him.
As I had forgotten my wallet, I had to go home to get it.
Since he's so tall, he drives a large car.
As her mother was ill, she couldn't leave the house.
Since he had no small change, he couldn't phone home.

50 F   ing-form or infinitive without "to"

> You'll see him eating breakfast.
> I sometimes hear people talking about it.
> I watched them rehearsing the play.

Nach Verben der sinnlichen Wahrnehmung (to see, to watch, to hear) steht in der Regel die ing-Form *(Ich beobachtete, wie sie probten)*. Will man ausdrücken, daß die Handlung beendet wurde, nimmt man den Infinitiv (ohne "to"): I watched them rehearse the play (d. h. ich blieb bis zum Ende).

Translate these sentences: ◯◯

Wir sahen, wie sie auf den Berg kletterten.   Ich beobachtete, daß er in das Haus ging.
Hörtest du, wie wir Walisisch redeten?   Ich hörte ihn, wie er die Treppe hinunterging.

50 G   Put these words in the correct order to make sentences: ◯◯

the / just / satellite / show / a low / from the Atlantic / pictures / coming in / approaching
today's / but / meeting / I expect / will be cancelled
practising / my arm / when / I broke / a new exercise
while / our viewers / eating / commercials / breakfast / don't want / just / to see
to be interrupted / my show / while / I don't like / rehearsing
there / any people / it / watching / if / the show / won't be / we don't improve / soon
he's / trying out / destroyed / his new gas cooker / just / the kitchen

50 H   Give the correct form of the verbs in brackets: ◯◯

Gilbert, an old friend of Humphrey's, (live) in Cornwall for many years
before he (return) to London.
By the end of next year you (finish) your studies.
He would enjoy the concert if he (be) here.
The police (find) Billy last night. He (run) away from home two days before.
You'll miss the train if you (not hurry).
If I (be) in your position, I would act differently.
I (just receive) a letter from Jane.
He (come to see) me this morning.
She (not finish) work yet.
What (you buy) yesterday?
When (you lose) your trumpet?
I (not see) him for three years.

50 I   What do these words from our story mean?

producer – correspondent – viewing figures – roving reporter – sub-titles – commercials

50 J   Pronunciation ◯◯

Write down the words that are pronounced as follows:

/njuːz/   /ɪntəˈrʌptɪd/   /ˈvjuːəz/   /straɪk/
/dɪˈstrɔɪd/   /ˈkænsld/   /əˈprəʊtʃɪŋ/   /klaɪm/
/hʌrɪ ˈʌp/   /ˈsɪtʃʊeɪtɪd/   /prɪˈzentə/   /ˈmenjuː/

50 K Winston Churchill (1874–1965) (CB)

When Churchill began to think about his career he couldn't make up his mind what he was going to be in life – should he become a soldier, a politician or a writer? He became all three. At the age of twenty he entered the British army and was sent to India as a soldier. Five years later he went to Africa as war correspondent for a London newspaper. He reported on the Boer War, became a prisoner of war and escaped. After returning to England, he decided to enter politics. In May 1940, Churchill became Prime Minister. In 1945 his Conservative party lost the elections, but he became Prime Minister again from 1951 to 1955.
He spent 60 years in the House of Commons, but found time to write more than two dozen books. For his historical works he was awarded the Nobel Prize for literature.

50 L *Try to write a curriculum vitae (Lebenslauf).*
Use participle constructions like "after attending ..., I went to ..."

50 M Situation – Say it in English

Sagen Sie, daß Sie abends gerne fernsehen.
Sagen Sie, daß Sie wünschten, es gäbe immer etwas in den Nachrichten,
das die Leute aufmuntert.
Sagen Sie, daß Sie enttäuscht sind, diese Nachricht zu hören.
Sagen Sie, daß Sie von Ihrem Kollegen heute noch keinen Bericht bekommen haben.
Sagen Sie, daß er eine Autopanne gehabt haben könnte.
Sagen Sie, daß es morgen keine Zeitungen geben wird, weil die Redakteure streiken.

There are no people like show people

50 N Summary 👂

Jim Cool, the presenter of "Breakfast Time", Windsor Television's popular breakfast show, was getting ready for his show. The producer interrupted him in the middle of his introduction, which annoyed Jim, as he hates being interrupted while rehearsing. He asked a girl sweeping the floor what she thought of the show. She said she sometimes heard people talking about it, but very few of them actually watched it. Jim asked her to get his breakfast, and started to discuss the day's show with the producer. Unfortunately there wasn't much news in the morning papers, so they had to ask their correspondents what was going on in their areas. But the industrial correspondent reporting from the Midlands couldn't be heard because of the noise of a factory in the background, and the cookery correspondent couldn't demonstrate any cooking because he'd destroyed the kitchen, trying out his new gas cooker. None of the other correspondents could send in a report either. Then Jim had an idea – they could show Jim Cool himself eating his breakfast!

Vocabulary **Wortschatz**

50	media	ˈmiːdɪə	Medien
	communications technology	kəmjuːnɪˈkeɪʃnz tekˈnɒlədʒɪ	Nachrichtentechnik
	to finance	tə faɪˈnæns	finanzieren
	possible	ˈpɒsəbl	möglich, denkbar
	public corporation	ˈpʌblɪk kɔːpəˈreɪʃn	öffentliche Körperschaft, Körperschaft des öffentlichen Rechts
	radio or television licence	ˈreɪdɪəʊ ɔː telɪˈvɪʒn laɪsəns	Lizenz für Hörfunk- und Fernsehempfänger
50 A	presenter	prɪˈzentə	(Fernseh-)Moderator(in)
	producer	prəˈdjuːsə	Produzent(in)
	cleaner	ˈkliːnə	Putzfrau
	cookery	ˈkʊkərɪ	Kochen, Kochkunst
	correspondent	kɒrɪˈspɒndənt	Korrespondent(in), Berichterstatter(in)
	racing	ˈreɪsɪŋ	Rennsport
	studio, pl -os	ˈstjuːdɪəʊ, ˈstjuːdɪəʊz	Studio, -os
	personality	pɜːsəˈnælətɪ	Persönlichkeit
	viewer	ˈvjuːə	Zuschauer(in)
	to be on the air	tə bɪ ɒn ðɪ ˈeə	senden (über Hörfunk bzw. Fernsehen)
	well-fed	ˈwel ˈfed	gut genährt
	industrial	ɪnˈdʌstrɪəl	Industrie-, industriell
	to try out	tə traɪ ˈaʊt	ausprobieren
	gas cooker	ˈgæs kʊkə	Gasofen
	on the course	ɒn ðə ˈkɔːs	auf dem Rennplatz
	satellite picture	ˈsætəlaɪt pɪktʃə	Satellitenbild

		deep depression	ˈdiːp dɪˈpreʃn	starkes Tiefdruckgebiet
		to approach	tʊ əˈprəʊtʃ	näherkommen
		viewing figures	ˈvjuːɪŋ fɪgəz	Zuschauerzahlen
		fitness expert	ˈfɪtnəs ekspɜːt	Gesundheits-Fachmann
		roving reporter	ˈrəʊvɪŋ rɪˈpɔːtə	reisender Reporter
		schoolmaster	ˈskuːlmɑːstə	Schullehrer
		sub-title	ˈsʌbtaɪtl	Untertitel
		to go on the air	tə ˈgəʊ ɒn ðɪ ˈeə	anfangen zu senden
		bank	bæŋk	Ufer
		edition	ɪˈdɪʃn	Ausgabe
50	H	to finish one's studies	tə ˈfɪnɪʃ wʌnz ˈstʌdɪz	sein Studium beenden
50	I	to contribute	tə kənˈtrɪbjuːt	beitragen
		caption	ˈkæpʃn	Untertitel, (erläuternder) Text
50	K	soldier	ˈsəʊldʒə	Soldat
		army	ˈɑːmɪ	Armee
		the Boer War	ðə ˈbɔː ˈwɔː	der Burenkrieg
		prisoner of war	ˈprɪznər əv ˈwɔː	Kriegsgefangener
		to escape	tʊ ɪˈskeɪp	fliehen
50	L	curriculum vitae	kəˈrɪkjʊləm ˈvaɪtɪ, kəˈrɪkjʊləm ˈviːtaɪ	Lebenslauf
50	N	to annoy	tʊ əˈnɔɪ	ärgern
		to sweep	tə ˈswiːp	kehren, fegen
		floor	flɔː	Fußboden
		to demonstrate	tə ˈdemənstreɪt	zeigen, vorführen

UNIT 51

(CB) The first Industrial Revolution caused a lot of men and women to become factory workers. They began to produce goods with the help of machines. In many industries this led to mass production, with the worker standing on an assembly line and carrying out one particular job over and over again.

After a time assembly line work was felt to be too monotonous and efforts were made to make it more human. Then the robot moved in. Today there are factories, especially in the vehicle industry, where all the manufacturing work is done automatically. This second Industrial Revolution threatens to take the worker out of his factory altogether. Robots do not need to strike for better pay or better working conditions. As more and more jobs are lost, new jobs have to be found in other fields. This has become today's problem number one. One thing is certain: the robot is here to stay. And if there is enough work to do, it will do it 24 hours a day and seven days a week!

51 A How a car is made

(J = Jane, R = Russell, C = Constance, B = Bright)

(Jane and Russell at home)

J What's happened, Russell? Have you been run over?

R No. I've been trying to get the car started.

J But it's just been serviced.

R I know that. Look! Brakes checked. Oil changed. Clutch repaired. But it won't start. Look at this!

J "We believe in the human touch!"

R The human touch! Look what the human touch has done to my car.

J	I think I know the answer to your problem. Look! "Human error eliminated. Made by robots, to be driven by people." That's a good slogan.
R	And that's an ordinary car.
J	Mm! Maybe. But it's not made by people. *And* I've been invited to visit the UK Motors factory.
R	Why?
J	I've been asked to write an article for *Technology News*. Come with me.

(at UK Motors Limited)

C	I'm Constance Smile, Public Relations Officer for UK Motors. Dr Bright, our Chief Designer, will be here in a moment. He's been delayed in the factory.
J	Oh, that's all right. We'll wait.
C	While you wait, you'll be shown a short history of the motor car. Now, in the early days cars were made like carriages. Each car was assembled by hand. Then came Henry Ford. He started mass production. The cars were made on a production line. Each worker did only one job at one stage of production. In this way, cars were made in less time and could be sold for less money. More cars were produced and more people owned cars. Since that time much progress has been made. New production methods have been introduced. Here, at UK Motors, the greatest improvements have been made in the last few years – since the arrival of Dr Bright.
B	I'm Edward Bright. Sorry I'm late. I was waiting for our new robot. It ought to be delivered today.
C	Dr Bright's arm was injured in an accident. It's been replaced by a special robot attachment.
B	Excuse me. This information has to be processed. I'm the only person here who understands it. Some of the robots understand it, of course.
C	We have a slogan – "What cannot be understood by a robot is not worth understanding."
B	Thank you, Miss Smile. You can describe the factory to our visitors while this information is being processed.
J	Is everything you need for the car manufactured in this factory?
C	Oh no. Some of the parts are bought from other firms – the tyres, for example. And the engines are made in another factory.
R	What about the steel?
C	The steel is brought here from the steel works. In this factory it is pressed into car bodies.
B	Pressed with precision, accuracy, perfection – by robots, my friends. We have a slogan – "Mistakes are made by men. Robots can do no wrong."
R	You have a lot of slogans, Dr Bright.
J	Er – can we see the factory?
C	Well, only certain parts of the factory can be visited.
B	The most important processes have to be kept secret. But don't worry. You'll see the cars being assembled. Don't be frightened. Come along. You'll be shown the various stages of the assembly process on our robot television screen.
J	Is all the assembly work done here?
C	Yes. All the parts are welded or put together.

B	And inspected and checked.
R	Who inspects and checks them?
B	No one. The checking is done automatically. Human beings can't be trusted to do such important work.
J	Do you trust people to do anything?
B	Oh, yes. They are given some jobs – not very important jobs.
C	Like public relations.
B	Exactly! You see, robots are more useful, more efficient than people. They don't get tired, they don't need to be given food. They can't be injured. *And* they can be programmed.
J	By computer?
B	Yes. Robots can be programmed to do what you want. What a pity human beings can't be programmed!
J	But what about you, Dr Bright? You designed these machines – these robots – and you're a human being.
C	Ah, but Dr Bright is different. He's the designer.
J	I suppose *somebody* must tell the machines what to do.
B	But soon the robots will be designed by other robots.
R	And what will the workers do? What will *you* do?
B	We shall all be replaced. People are being replaced every day. Look!
R	What's happening to them?
B	They're being sent home. They're not needed in the factory. They've been replaced. But I shall be needed for some time.
J	What happens here?
C	The cars are painted in this part of the factory. Then they are tested.
B	Would you like to ride in a car that is being tested?
J	Er – no, thank you. I'd prefer to watch.
B	All right. I shall start the test.
R	Hey! There's no one in the car.
B	Of course not. When it's tested, the car is driven by a robot. A very small robot.
J	It's being driven fast.
C	Oh dear!
R	One of your robots has been destroyed, I think.
B	Oh, no. The robot will be safe. In a crash like that, the car would be damaged, human beings would be hurt or killed. But robots would not be harmed.
C	Wouldn't you like a car like that, Mr Grant?
R	No, thanks. I'll keep the one I've got.

(the telephone in Dr Bright's robot arm rings)

B	Answer that please, Miss Smile.
C	Hello, Constance Smile speaking. Yes. Yes. I'll tell Dr Bright. The new robot has been delivered.
B	Good!
C	It isn't what you expected. It's been sent to replace you.
B	But I can't be replaced. Not yet.
C	Sorry, Dr Bright. You *have* been replaced. That was the robot speaking on the phone.

51 B Questions

What are Jane and Russell visiting?
Who is Dr Bright?
Why was Dr Bright delayed?
What happened to Dr Bright's arm?
What is the advantage of a robot over a human worker?
What happened to Dr Bright at the end of the story?
Who built the first American car?
Why are many people afraid of robots?

51 C And you?

What machines do you work with?
Could a robot do your work?
What will happen to human brains and jobs if more and more computers are used in industry?

51 D Passive (III) — Passiv

Übersicht

Präsens	The steel is brought here from the steel works.	*wird gebracht*
einfache Vergangenheit	Each car was assembled by hand.	*wurde montiert*
Perfekt	His arm has been replaced by a special robot attachment.	*ist ersetzt worden*
Vorvergangenheit	Dr Bright had been warned.	*war gewarnt worden*
Futur	We will all be replaced.	*werden ersetzt werden*
	Who is going to be replaced?	*wird ersetzt werden*
Futur Perfekt	Dr Bright will have been replaced by the end of this month.	*wird ersetzt worden sein*
unvollständige Hilfsverben		
can	Robots can't be injured.	*können nicht verletzt werden*
could	The cars could be sold for less money.	*könnten verkauft werden*
have to	This information has to be processed.	*muß verarbeitet werden*
ought to should	It ought to be (= should be) delivered today.	*sollte geliefert werden*

Verlaufsform Präsens	The car is being tested.	*wird gerade getestet*
einfache Vergangenheit	People were being replaced.	*wurden ersetzt*
persönliches Passiv	You'll be shown a robot.	*Man wird Ihnen ... zeigen.*
	I was given a job.	*Mir wurde ... gegeben.*

Das Passiv kommt besonders häufig in Sachtexten vor, wie z. B. der Beschreibung technischer Vorgänge.

Bei passiven Verbformen behält die Präposition ihren Platz hinter dem Verb: I hate being laughed at. He's been taken to hospital and he's already been operated on.

51 E Change the sentences into the passive:

You shouldn't allow them to smoke.
We can't test the cars.
They've bought the tyres from a different factory.
A careless driver was driving the car.
We'll invite you to visit our factory.
Someone was processing the information.
We must look into this matter.
She told him to be quick.
In the early days they made cars like carriages.
Each worker did only one job at one stage of production.
Human beings, not robots, make mistakes.
They've found your wallet.
They're sending him abroad.
They'll look after you.
Somebody must do something for the poor.
People play football all over the world.

51 F Put the verbs in the correct form:

Last year he (spend) two weeks in the USA. All his expenses (pay) by his firm.
Brooklyn Bridge (design) by a German architect.
In 1982 the Barbican Centre (officially open) by Queen Elizabeth II.
The Sears Tower in Chicago (say) to be the tallest skyscraper in the world.
My car (tow away) yesterday.
Any car causing an obstruction can (tow away) by the police.

Jane and Russell (travel) to Munich by plane. They (pick up) at the airport by car.
During the conference Senator Gatewater (interrupt) several times by his secretary.
David Copperfield (write) by Charles Dickens.
That bridge (build) by next Christmas.

51 G Put in the missing preposition:

The assembly work is done here. All the parts are put …
Do you think robots can be relied …?
He was taken no notice …
The doctor was sent …
She has never been heard … again.
This statement has been objected …
What is he being accused …?
The problem ought to be dealt … next time.
The forms have to be filled …
He was run … by a car.

51 H Jane's article for "Technology News"

Human Error Eliminated

Last week I was given a chance to visit the UK Motors factory. It is amazing how production methods have changed since the first robots were introduced. They are becoming more and more reliable and efficient. Robots are being used not only for assembling cars but also for inspecting and checking them. Even when the cars are being tested they are driven by a robot.

The managers, of course, are in favour of these robots because they don't come in late, they don't get tired, they can't be injured, they can't fall ill, and they don't claim higher wages. They expect robots to increase industrial production.

These electronic workers are about to revolutionise society.

51 I Explain the following expressions:

robot – error – to assemble cars – a chance – to visit – efficient – to increase

51 J *Translate the article in 51 H into German*

51 K Letter writing

Invent a letter that Jane might write to the Public Relations Officer.
Use these expressions:

thank you – opportunity to visit the factory – impressed by your robots – it is amazing what these machines can do – hope that workers who are replaced by robots will be offered retraining for other work

51 L Situation – Say it in English

Sie besichtigen eine Autofabrik.
Fragen Sie, ob die Karosserien hier gebaut werden.
Ihr Gesprächspartner sagt, daß die Karosserien bereits fertig von einer Firma in Sheffield gekauft werden.
Fragen Sie, ob die Autos hier montiert werden.
Ihr Gesprächspartner sagt, daß die gesamte Montierarbeit in dieser Werkstatt gemacht wird.
Fragen Sie, ob die Autos hier lackiert werden.
Ihr Gesprächspartner sagt, daß mehrere Lackierungen (coats of paint) vorgenommen werden.
Fragen Sie, wo die Autos getestet werden.
Ihr Gesprächspartner sagt, daß die Autos von Robotern getestet werden.
Fragen Sie, wieviele Autos pro Woche hier hergestellt werden.
Ihr Gesprächspartner sagt etwa 500, ein Drittel davon wird innerhalb Großbritanniens verkauft, zwei Drittel werden exportiert.

51 M Summary ◯◯

Russell had just collected his car from the garage, where he had had it serviced. But it still wouldn't start. Jane showed him a brochure about "the car of the future", with the slogan "Made by robots, to be driven by people". She asked Russell to go with her on a visit to UK Motors – she'd been asked to write an article for a magazine. The Public Relations Officer at UK Motors, Miss Constance Smile, welcomed them to the ultra-modern factory, and while they waited for Dr Bright, the Chief Designer, she showed them a short history of the motor car, from the days when each car was assembled by hand, up to today's robot-operated factories. Dr Bright arrived, and Miss Smile explained that his right arm had been replaced by a robot, as it had been injured in an accident. Dr Bright apologised for being late, and said he'd been waiting for their new robot to be delivered. He went off to process some information on a computer, and Miss Smile talked to Jane and Russell about the factory. She said not all the parts for the cars were made there; in fact quite a lot were made in other factories. Dr Bright explained that the people who worked in the factory were gradually being replaced by robots, which didn't get tired, couldn't be injured, and didn't need to be fed. Suddenly the telephone in Dr Bright's robot arm rang. Miss Smile answered it – it was the new robot speaking! It had arrived, and Dr Bright himself had been replaced!

Don't lose your head

Vocabulary **Wortschatz**

51	mass production	ˈmæs prəˈdʌkʃn	Massenproduktion, -fertigung
	assembly line	əˈsemblɪ laɪn	Fließband
	to carry out	tə kærɪ ˈaʊt	ausführen, ausüben
	one particular job	ˈwʌn pəˈtɪkjʊlə ˈdʒɒb	ein einzelner Arbeitsgang, eine einzelne Arbeit
	monotonous	məˈnɒtənəs	eintönig, monoton
	human	ˈhjuːmən	menschlich
	robot	ˈrəʊbɒt	Roboter
	to move in	tə muːv ˈɪn	einziehen
	vehicle industry	ˈvɪəkl ɪndəstrɪ	Fahrzeugindustrie
	to threaten	tə ˈθretn	drohen
	altogether	ɔːltəˈgeðə	ganz und gar, völlig
51 A	touch	tʌtʃ	Empfindung, Gefühl; Spur, Note
	human error eliminated	ˈhjuːmən ˈerər ɪˈlɪmɪneɪtɪd	menschlicher Irrtum ausgeschlossen
	slogan	ˈsləʊgən	Werbespruch, Wahlspruch, Motto
	public relations officer	ˈpʌblɪk rɪˈleɪʃnz ˈɒfɪsə	Pressechef(in)
	chief designer	ˈtʃiːf dɪˈzaɪnə	Chefkonstrukteur
	carriage	ˈkærɪdʒ	Kutsche, Wagen
	to assemble	tʊ əˈsembl	zusammenbauen, montieren
	production line	prəˈdʌkʃn laɪn	Fließband
	one stage of production	ˈwʌn ˈsteɪdʒ əv prəˈdʌkʃn	eine Produktionsphase, ein Produktionsabschnitt
	improvement	ɪmˈpruːvmənt	Verbesserung
	to deliver	tə dɪˈlɪvə	liefern
	attachment	əˈtætʃmənt	(Zusatz-)Vorrichtung
	to process information	tə ˈprəʊses ɪnfəˈmeɪʃn	Informationen verarbeiten
	tyre	taɪə	Reifen
	steel	stiːl	Stahl
	steel works	ˈstiːl wɜːks	Stahlwerk, -fabrik
	to press	tə ˈpres	pressen
	car body	ˈkɑː bɒdɪ	Karosserie
	precision	prɪˈsɪʒn	Genauigkeit
	accuracy	ˈækjʊrəsɪ	Genauigkeit, Sorgfalt
	perfection	pəˈfekʃn	Vollkommenheit
	process	ˈprəʊses	(Produktions-)Verfahren
	to keep secret	tə ˈkiːp ˈsiːkrət	geheimhalten
	assembly process	əˈsemblɪ prəʊses	Montageverfahren
	screen	skriːn	Bildschirm
	to weld together	tə ˈweld təˈgeðə	zusammenschweißen
	to trust s.b.	tə ˈtrʌst	jdm. (ver)trauen, sich verlassen auf jdn.
	to program(me)	tə ˈprəʊgræm	programmieren
	to design	tə dɪˈzaɪn	entwerfen
	to harm	tə ˈhɑːm	verletzen, wehtun, schädigen

51 C	brain(s)	breɪn(z)	(Ge-)Hirn
51 F	expenses	ɪkˈspensɪz	Ausgaben, Aufwendungen
51 H	reliable	rɪˈlaɪəbl	zuverlässig
	to be in favour of s.th.	tə bi ɪn ˈfeɪvər əv	für etwas sein, für etwas eintreten
	to fall ill	tə fɔːl ˈɪl	krank werden
	to claim	tə ˈkleɪm	fordern
	to revolutionise	tə revəˈluːʃənaɪz	umwandeln, verändern
51 L	coat of paint	ˈkəʊt əv ˈpeɪnt	Lackierung
	to apply	tʊ əˈplaɪ	anwenden
	to export	tʊ ɪkˈspɔːt, tʊ ˈekspɔːt	exportieren
51 M	to welcome	tə ˈwelkəm	begrüßen
	ultra-modern	ˈʌltrə ˈmɒdn	höchst modern
	robot-operated factory	ˈrəʊbɒt ɒpəreɪtɪd ˈfæktərɪ	von Robotern betriebene Fabrik
	gradually	ˈɡrædʒʊəlɪ	allmählich, nach und nach
	to feed, fed, fed	tə ˈfiːd, fed, fed	füttern

Wortschatzregister

Die Zahlen verweisen auf die entsprechenden Abschnitte in den Units, in denen ein Wort oder Ausdruck in einer bestimmten Bedeutung zum erstenmal vorkommt.

Abkürzungen:
S = Substantiv
Adj = Adjektiv
V = Verb
pl = Plural

A

abroad 44
academic 42K
accent 41N
accompany 48M
accuracy 51A
accuse (V) 45G
accustomed to 45D
acknowledge (V) 45G
across 41A
adjust (V) 47A
adopt (V) 46K
adult (Adj) 42C
adventure 42M
advice 41A
agreement 40A
ahead of 40A
aim at (V) 45N
air 50A
alert 48A
alias 41A
allowance 44M
alltogheter 51
amused 47N
annoy (V) 50N
annoyed 44O
anteroom 45A
apply (V) 51L
appreciate (V) 40D
approach (V) 50A
approximate 48A
arch 48
archaeologist 48
arise, arose, arisen (V) 46
armed robbery 41A
army 50K
around 41A
arrange (V) 41N
arrangement 46A
assassin 40K
assemble (V) 51A

assembly line 51
association 46K
astonished at 45D
attachment 51A
attemd to (V) 47A
attendant 41A
attraction 42
avoid (V) 40D
award (V) 42M

B

bachelor's degree 42J
baggage 42L
ballet 43
bandaged 48A
bank 48, 50A
barkeepere 49Q
barrister 45
based on 40
baseball 42A
basketball 42A
battery 47A
beat (S) 48A
beat, beat, beaten (V) 44A
beef 41K
BC = before Christ 48
benefit 44M
beside 48G
best-seller 42M
beyond 48A
bill 41I
biscuit 40A
bite (S) 45A
bitter (Adj) 46M
block (S) 41
block (V) 42A
boom 42
brain(s) 51C
brakes 47G
branch 40
break (S) 45A
Breton (S + Adj) 47L
brilliant 43A
bring down (V) 46
brind up (V) 43L
bump into (V) 41N
buried 40K
business adminstration 42A

C

cab 41A
cafeteria 42A
campus 42A
candy, pl candies 42L
can't help 40D
can't stand 40D
captain 49A
caption 50I
car body 51A
car registration number 48A
care about (V) 40D
carriage 51A
carry on (V) 40A
carry out (V) 51
case 41D
cash 41A
cemetery 40K
central area 42
chain 41E
champion 49A
characteristics 42M
check (S) 41A
checkup (S) 44
cheerful 43M
cheerio 41A
cheerleader 42A
chemist's 42L
chicken 41K
chief designer 51A
childhood 46M
china 47
Chinese (S + Adj) 42
cirle 48
circular 48
civil war 42M
claim (S) 48A
claim (V) 51H
clay 47
cleaner 50A
clearly 43A
cliff 47
climate 47
close 48A
closed shop 46K
club 49
clue 44A
coast 42

coat of paint 51L
coke 41A
college 42J
colour 45A
comedy 43
commit (V) 41B
communications 50
compete (V) 46
complete (V) 42J
compulsory 44M
concentrate on (V) 40D
conditions 41G
confusion 49
Congress 40
constable 48A
construct (V) 48B
contents 41A
continue (V) 40H
contribute (V) 50I
conversation 46B
cookery 50A
cookie 40A
Cornish 47L
corporation 50
correspondent 40K
counter 41A
countryside 46C
course 50A
court 40
crash 48M
crash helmet 43A
crazy 41A
criminal (S) 41A
criminal court 45
critic 43A
criticism 43M
crossword (puzzle) 44A
cure (S) 44O
curriculum vitae 50L
cycle (V) 48A
cyclist 48A

D

damage (S) 45A
dance (V) 45E
dartboard 49
darts 49
deadly 43A
deep 50A
defence 40A
defense 40A
deli(catessen) 41A
deliver (V) 51A

delivery 46J
Democrats 40
demolish (V) 45
demonstrate (V) 50N
demonstration 46A
dental surgery 44O
dentist 44
deny (V) 40A
depend on (V) 41K
depression 50A
description 41A
design (V) 51A
desolate 48
despatch department 46J
destroy (V) 42
detect (V) 48A
detest (V) 40D
dicitionary 43H
dining-hall 45A
direct (V) 43A
direction 41
director 43A
dish 41K
dissatisfied 46B
disturb (V) 40A
ditch 48
divide (V) 40
drama school 43L
dramatic 43A
dramatist 43K
draw (V) 48A
dreadful 43A
drill (S) 44A
drill (V) 44A
drugstore 42L
due to 46K
duty 48A

E

earthquake 42
eclipse 48
edition 50A
educational system 42C
efficient 46A
elementary school 42J
eliminated 51A
empire 46
employed 46K
enclose (V) 46J
ending 41J
engine-house 47
enter (V) 40K
enterprise 46K

entirely 45M
environment 42M
error 41G
escape (V) 50K
even 40A
eventually 43M
evil 43A
Executive branch 40
exhaust (S) 47A
exhaust pipe 47A
expectation 46M
expenses 51F
experienced 48A
export (V) 51L

F

factory 46
fail (V) 46
faint (V) 48E
fair 41A
fairly 49A
fall down (V) 41D
fall ill (V) 51H
fall off (V) 47A
fast food 41F
father-in-law 44A
in favour of 51H
federal 40
Federal Bureau of
    Investigation (FBI) 40A
feed, fed, fed (V) 51M
feeling 43A
fellow 45A
fellow citizen 40K
female 44B
field 41E
finance (V) 50
fine (S) 45C
fitness expert 50A
fix (V) 47A
floor 50N
fond of 45D
for God's sake(s) 42A
forced 44A
foreign affairs 40B
fortune 42M
fraternity 42A
freshman 42A
frighten away (V) 44A
frightened of 48A
frontrunner 40A
fumes 47A
further 48A

G

gain (V) 40
gains 46O
gallery 40A
gas cooker 50A
gas(oline) 42L
gateway 42
gather (V) 42A
gear 42A
gee 40A
general meeting 46A
general practitioner 44
gentle 47
get hold of (V) 41A
get tired (V) 40A
ghost 43A
give rise (V) 47
go abroad (V) 44
gold rush 42
good-humoured 42M
Governor 40
grade 42A
gradually 51M
grandparents 44L
grandson 44L
gravely 40L
grounds 42K
group practice 44
guess (V) 41A
Gulf Stream 47
gun 41A
gunpoint 41A

H

habit 45F
hair 41A
hamburger 41K
handbook 47A
handle (V) 41A
hang up (V) 42A
harm (V) 51A
head (V) 40
healthy 41A
helicopter 40A
help out (V) 42A
high school 42A
hill 40A
historian 48
hold office (V) 40L
hold, held, held up (V) 44A
hold-up 41A
honour (V) 43A
honourable 41A

horrified 43M
hostile 42M
House of Representatives 40
human 51
humorist 42M

I

ice-hockey 42J
illegal 47A
immortal 43A
import (V) 40A
improvement 51A
inaugural address 40K
incident 48A
indicate (V) 48A
industrial correspondent 50A
inflation 46
influence 47A
inhabitant 42
injection 44A
injured 48F
injury 48A
inn 45
Inns of Court 45
inspect (V) 47A
institution 43
insurance 44M
insure (V) 48A
insured 48A
intelligent 44G
interruption 40A
interview (V) 40A
introduce (V) 40
introduction 47J
investigate (V) 41D
involved in 45C
issue (V) 41A

J

judge 45A
Judicial branch 40
junior 42A
junior clerk 46M
justice 45

K

keen on 45D
keep an eye on (V) 41A
keep away from (V) 41A
keep secret (V) 51A

kick (V) 47N
knights 47
knock (V) 41A
knock down (V) 48A
knock over (V) 49A
knowledge 41D

L

lamp post 48A
landscape 47
law 45
lawyer 45
lead (V) 43
leather 41J
legal 45
Legislative branch 40
license (S) 50
licensing hours 49
licensing laws 49
lieutenant 41A
light (V) 44A
lightning strike 46A
limit (V) 40
line 41A, 43A
in line with 40
lining (S) 47N
liquor store 41A
local news 41A
lord 41A

M

magnificent 42
maintenance 47A
major (Adj) 46
make sure (V) 46A
manager 46A
manual 47A
manufacture (V) 40A
march in (V) 46A
market 46
marriage 42I
mass production 51
matter of fact 42A
meal 45B
measurement 43J
media 50
medical register 44A
melodrama 43A
message 43A
metropolis 42
Mexican (S + Adj) 42
Midsummer Day 48
Midwinter Day 48

mild 47
mime (V) 42A
mind (S) 45A
mine (S) 47
minister 40A
modernise (V) 46
monotonous 51
moon 47
motorbike 43M
mousetrap 43
move (V) 41A
move in (V) 51
multicultural 42
murder trial 45
musical 43A

N

National Assistance
 Board 44M
negotiate (V) 46A
negotiation 43J
neither 44A
newscaster 41A
nickname 41
nil 44A
nominate (V) 40K
noon 41A
novel 42M
nuclear weapons 44E
number (V) 41

O

object to (V) 40D
obstruction 48A
old-age pension 44M
open air 47A
opportunity 45F
in order to 49A
origin 49B
originate (V) 45B
otherwise 41A
ouch 44A
outskirts 40K
overhear (V) 46O
overnight 42
overseas 46
overtake (V) 45A
overtime 44A

P

pack (V) 47A
packing 46J
pains 45O
pair 41A
palm tree 47
pants 41D
pardon (V) 40D
parents-in-law 44L
participate (V) 42M
particluar 51
pavement 42L
pedestrian crossing 40A
pen name 42M
penalty 41C
peninsula 47
perfection 51A
period 40B
personality 50A
pick up (V) 44G
pickpocket 41M
pilot 42M
placard 46A
plain (S) 48
poison (S) 47J
poison (V) 47A
political science 40K
pollute (V) 47A
pollution 47J
possible 50
postal order 46J
pottery 47
practice (V) 40D
practise (V) 40D
precinct 41A
precision 51A
predict (V) 48
present (V) 43A
presenter 50A
press (V) 51A
prevent (V) 40
prevention 44O
previous 47N
principle 40
prisoner of war 50K
process (S) 51A
process (V) 51A
producer 50A
production 43
production line 51A
profit 46
program(me) (V) 51A
progress 41D
prohibit (V) 44A
proud of 45D

provide (V) 44M
public relations officer 51A
publish (V) 41G
pull out (V) 44A
put forward (V) 48
pyramid-shaped 47

Q

quotation 40K

R

race 40A
racing 50A
raise (V) 42M
rate 46C
raw material 46
real estate 41A
rebuild (V) 44E
receipt 46J
re-elect (V) 40
reflect (V) 42M
rehearsal 43A
rehearse (V) 43A
reliable 51H
relish 42A
rely on (V) 40D
remove (V) 43A
renew (V) 47B
report (V) 44A
Republicans 40
resort 47
revolutionise (V) 51H
rewrite (V) 43A
ride (V) 48M
ridiculous 43A
ring back (V) 46A
risk 45F
robbery 41A
robot 51
robot-operated 51M
rocky 47
role 46
romance 47
romantic 41A
room-mate 42A
rough 41A
routine 44C
roving reporter 50A
rules 49A
run for (V) 40A
run-down 41N
rush (V) 42
rye 41A

119

S

satellite picture 50A
schoolmaster 50A
scissors 41D
score (S) 49Q
score (V) 49
scratch 45A
screen 51 A
seafood 41K
secretary 40A
Secretary of State 40A
seem (V) 41N
self-employed 44
Senate 40
Senator 40A
senior 42A
sentence 42M
service (V) 47A
set (V) 46A
set (S) 46J
setting (Adj) 48
shake (S) 42A
shaken 48A
shine, shone, shone (V) 48
ship 42M
shoot (V) 43A
shop steward 46A
shoplift (V) 41J
short story 42M
show in (V) 40A
sickness 44M
sidewalk 42L
sidewalk café 41K
silent 41A
silver 47N
sister-in-law 44L
site 40
sketch 46M
slogan 51A
smell (V) 47A
smoke (S) 47A
smoked 41K
smoothly 47A
snack 41K
social 49
society 43A
soft 44A
soldier 50K
solicitor 46M
sophomore 42A
sorority 42A
sound (S) 44A
southwesterly 47
spanner 47A
sparking plugs 47A

specially 41A
spectacles 41A
spiced 41K
split (V) 41A
spoil (V) 46C
sports 42A
stage 51A
stairs 41A
standard (Adj) 49
standard (S) 46K
stare (V) 48A
statement 48A
steel 51A
steel works 51A
stimulator 42K
stock 44A
stock market 41A
stone 48
streetcar 42L
strike, struck, struck (V) 48A
struggle 42M
studies pl 50H
studio 50A
stuffy 45A
style 42M
subscription 46K
sub-title 50A
substract (V) 49
succeed in (V) 40A
such 40A
suggestion 40G
sunglasses 46E
supply (V) 46
support (S) 40A
Supreme Court 40
surgery 44O
surprised 49F
surrounded 41
suspicious 48A
sustain (V) 48A
sweep (V) 50N
sweets 42L

T

take care (V) 41A
take down (V) 48A
take in (V) 41A
take place (V) 40B
task 46K
teabreak 46A
temple 48
term 40
terms 41A
theory 48

therefore 46K
thorough 44A
threaten (V) 51
thriving 42
throw (V) 49A
tin 47
tip 47
tooth, pl teeth 44A
toothache 44N
torture (V) 44A
touch (S) 51A
tourism 47
tow away (V) 47A
towards 44
trade (V) 46
trade agreement 40A
Trade Secretary 40A
trade union 46K
Trades Union Congress 46K
tragedy 43K
train (V) 42A
tram 42L
transform (V) 42
transportation 41A
tray 42A
treat (V) 44A
trend 44
trial 45
trilithon 48
triple 49A
trolley 46A
tropical plant 47
trust (V) 51A
try out (V) 50A
tune (V) 47A
tyre 51A

U

ultra-modern 51M
understanding 48A
unemployed 41E
unemployment benefit 44M
unhealthy 47A
union 46A
United Nations 41
untrained recruits 48A
uptown 41A
use 40A

V

vacation 41A
various 42

vehicle 47A
vehicle industry 51
viewer 50A
viewing figures 50A
villain 43A
visa 47E

W

wages 44I
waitress 41A
warm (V) 47

waterfront 42M
way 45F
weaken (V) 46K
weapon 44E
welcome (V) 51M
weld together (V) 51A
welfare 44M
well-fed 50A
wharf, pl wharves 42
whatever 49L
whenever 49L
whereupon 47N
whether 40
whoever 49L

wish (V) 46
witness (V) 48A
wooded 47
worker 46A
worry about (V) 40D
wounded 40K
wrist 48 A

Y

yacht 48F
yeah 40A

Aussprachehilfen zu Eigennamen

Albert	ˈælbət	Lincoln	ˈlɪŋkən
Arnold	ˈɑːnəld	Jack London	ˈdʒæk ˈlʌndən
King Arthur	kɪŋ ˈɑːθə	Long Hall	ˈlɒŋ ˈhɔːl
John Benson	ˈdʒɒn ˈbensn	Macbeth	məkˈbeθ
Bloomingdale	ˈbluːmɪŋdeɪl	Magic Flute	ˈmædʒɪk ˈfluːt
Edward Bright	ˈedwəd ˈbraɪt	Metropolitan Opera	metrəˈpɒlɪtən ˈɒpərə
Julius Caesar	ˈdʒuːliəs ˈsiːzə	Mission Dolores	ˈmɪʃn ˈdɒlərəs, dəˈlɔːrɪs
Agatha Christie	ˈægəθə ˈkrɪsti	Royal Oak	ˈrɔɪəl ˈəʊk
Christmas Carol	ˈkrɪsməs ˈkærəl	O. Henry	ˈəʊ ˈhenrɪ
Winston Churchill	ˈwɪnstən ˈtʃɜːtʃɪl	Othello	əˈθeləʊ
Commonwealth	ˈkɒmənwelθ	Pastrami	pəˈstrɑːmɪ
Jim Cool	ˈdʒɪm ˈkuːl	Pickwick Papers	ˈpɪkwɪk ˈpeɪpəz
David Copperfield	ˈdeɪvɪd ˈkɒpəfiːld	Pilkington Booth ffrench	ˈpɪlkɪŋtən ˈbuːð ˈfrentʃ
Robinson Crusoe	ˈrɒbɪnsn ˈkruːsəʊ		
Daniel Defoe	ˈdænjəl dɪˈfəʊ	William Sidney Porter	ˈwɪljəm ˈsɪdnɪ ˈpɔːtə
Charles Dickens	ˈtʃɑːlz ˈdɪkɪnz	Purcell	ˈpɜːsl, pɜːˈsel
Elizabeth	ɪˈlɪzəbəθ	Richard	ˈrɪtʃəd
Huckleberry Finn	ˈhʌklbərɪ ˈfɪn	Rockefeller	ˈrɒkəfelə
Avery Fisher	ˈeɪvərɪ ˈfɪʃə	Romeo and Juliet	ˈrəʊmɪəʊ ən ˈdʒuːlɪet
Henry Ford	ˈhenrɪ ˈfɔːd	Tom Sawyer	ˈtɒm ˈsɔɪə, ˈsɔːjə
Frenchie	ˈfrentʃɪ	Lauren Schmidt	ˈlɒrən ˈʃmɪt
Gatewater	ˈɡeɪtwɔːtə	Constance Smile	ˈkɒnstəns ˈsmaɪl
Gilbert	ˈɡɪlbət	Tristan and Isolde	ˈtrɪstən ənd ɪˈzɒldə
Gray's Inn	ˈɡreɪz ˈɪn	Turpin	ˈtɜːpɪn
Hamlet	ˈhæmlɪt	Mark Twain	ˈmɑːk ˈtweɪn
Anne Hathaway	ˈæn ˈhæθəweɪ	Oliver Twist	ˈɒlɪvə ˈtwɪst
Heelstone	ˈhiːlstəʊn	United Nations	juːˈnaɪtɪd ˈneɪʃnz
Ernest Hemingway	ˈɜːnɪst ˈhemɪŋweɪ	George Washington	ˈdʒɔːdʒ ˈwɒʃɪŋtən
Henry James	ˈhenrɪ ˈdʒeɪmz	Weekend Chronicle	ˈwiːkend ˈkrɒnɪkl
Trevor Jones	ˈtrevə ˈdʒəʊnz	Wyford	ˈwaɪfəd
King Lear	kɪŋ ˈlɪə		

Aussprachehilfen zu Orts- und Ländernamen

Arlington	ˈɑːlɪŋtən	Land's End	ˈlændz ˈend
Asia	ˈeɪʃə	Lexington	ˈleksɪŋtən
Australia	ɒˈstreɪljə	Mevagissey	mevəˈgɪsi
Berkeley	*(BE)* ˈbɑːklɪ	Midlands	ˈmɪdləndz
	(AE) ˈbɜːklɪ	Mousehole	ˈmaʊzl
Boston	ˈbɒstən	Newgate	ˈnjuːgɪt
Brazil	brəˈzɪl	New Jersey	njuːˈdʒɜːzɪ
Bude	bjuːd	Newlyn	njuːˈlɪn
California	kælɪˈfɔːnjə	Oakland Bay Bridge	ˈəʊklənd beɪ ˈbrɪdʒ
Capitol Hill	ˈkæpɪtl ˈhɪl	Old Bailey	əʊld ˈbeɪlɪ
Chinatown	ˈtʃaɪnətaʊn	Penzance	penˈzæns
Columbia	kəˈlʌmbɪə	Polperro	ˈpəʊlperəʊ
Columbus Circle	kəˈlʌmbəs ˈsɜːkl	Royal Albert Hall	ˈrɔɪəl ˈælbət ˈhɔːl
Cornwall	ˈkɔːnwəl	Royal Festival Hall	ˈrɔɪəl ˈfestɪvl ˈhɔːl
Dallas	ˈdæləs	St. Austell	snt ˈɔːstl
Golden Gate Bridge	ˈgəʊldən ˈgeɪt ˈbrɪdʒ	St. Ives	snt ˈaɪvz
Grand Central Station	ˈgrænd ˈsentrəl ˈsteɪʃn	Salisbury	ˈsɔːlzbərɪ
Harvard	ˈhɑːvəd	Stonehenge	stəʊnˈhendʒ
Hudson River	ˈhʌdsn ˈrɪvə	Texas	ˈteksəs
Japan	dʒəˈpæn	Tintagel	tɪnˈtædʒl
Kempton Park	ˈkemtən ˈpɑːk	Wiltshire	ˈwɪltʃə
Klondike	ˈklɒndaɪk		

Erklärung der grammatischen Bezeichnungen

verwendete Bezeichnung	englische Bezeichnung	weitere Bezeichnung
Absichtssätze	clauses of purpose	Nebensätze der Absicht und des Zweckes
bestimmter Artikel	definite article	
unbestimmter Artikel	indefinite article	
Gradadverbien	adverbs of degree	
indirekte Befehle	reported imperative	
indirekte Fragen	reported questions	
indirekte Rede	reported speech	
Infinitiv mit "to"	to-infinitive	to-Form
Infinitiv ohne "to"	infinitive without "to"	Grundform
ing-Form	ing-form	Gerund(ium)
Nebensatz	sub(ordinate)-clause	
Objekt	object	Ergänzung
Partizip Präsens	present participle	Mittelwort der Gegenwart
Partizip Perfekt	past participle	Mittelwort der Vergangenheit
Partizipialsätze	participle clauses	participial clauses
Passiv	passive (voice)	Leideform
Plural	plural	Mehrzahl
Singular	singular	Einzahl

Key to the Exercises
Schlüssel zu den Übungen

Unit 40

40 B The Senate and the House of Representatives.
It's called "Congress".
It's in the Capitol.
It's the White House.
He can be re-elected once. (… for a second term.)
Presidential elections take place (are) every four years.
The Democrats and the Republicans.
It's the Governor.
There are one hundred Senators, two for each state.
They are elected for a six-year term; one third of them is elected every two years.
He's called "Secretary of State".

40 E I'm sure you'll soon succeed in speaking English fluently.
Don't prevent him from learning.
I've given up smoking.
It's no use saying that I enjoyed it.
We thought of driving across the States. (We thought about …)
People don't mind queueing in front of the White House.
Someone suggested going out for lunch.
Would you mind closing the window?
It's a pleasure being in Washington. (It's a pleasure to be …)
I don't object to working on Sundays.
It's no use trying to find excuses.

40 G Do you mind me making a suggestion?
I don't like her interrupting the conference.
Please excuse us calling you by your first name.
She doesn't like him coming late every time.
You must forgive us interrupting him.
Fancy him living with us for six months.
I remember them forgetting to come to our party.
We can't understand you walking through Central Park alone.

40 I What do you intend to do today? (… doing today?)
I'd love to come and see you.
He'd like to drink a glass of wine.
I enjoy travelling.
Some people hate queueing. (… to queue)
I prefer walking. (… to walk)
She doesn't mind being disturbed while she's working.

40 J
to disturb	–	to interrupt
it's nice	–	it's a pleasure
biscuit	–	cookie
to produce	–	to manufacture

40 K The man in question was John F. Kennedy.

40 L gravely wounded
He reported on a conference.
A period of time in which the President holds office.
A person who kills a politician.
the suburbs of Washington
inaugural speech

40 M Excuse me, can you tell me the way to the White House?
How long does it take to get there?
It's about half an hour's walk.
Can I visit the White House?
There's always a long queue in front of the White House.
Thank you for warning me.
I don't mind queueing.

Unit 41

41 B She's a police officer (a policewoman, a lieutenant).
He committed armed robbery (a robbery).
He held up a liquor store.
They know that he's a well-known London criminal.
He took five thousand dollars.
He described Frenchie as tall with fair hair.

41 E That's an interesting piece of information.
Could you give me a pair of scissors, please?
These glasses (spectacles) are old-fashioned. (This pair of glasses is …)
The United States has a large number of unemployed.
I'll give you a useful piece of advice.
Can you bring the furniture tomorrow?
Many thanks for the information.
He bought three pairs of jeans yesterday at Bloomingdale's.
I'd like to see the contents of your wallet.
Much progress has been made in the field of technology.

41 F I haven't seen you here before.
The police are looking for a man who held up a liquor store last night and took $5,000.
The police have issued the following description.
Humphrey has never climbed the Empire State Building.
Fast food chains have reached Europe now.
She went to the Metropolitan Museum last Friday.
In our last programme Jane interviewed a Senator.
There was an excellent performance of "The Magic Flute" yesterday evening in the Metropolitan Opera House.

41 G A counter is a table where customers are served or goods are shown.
Terms are conditions.
To split means to divide.
To take somebody in means to arrest somebody.
A mistake is an error.
To issue means to publish.

41 H seat – actually – holiday – Wall Street – a piece of advice – tomorrow – take care – clothes – cash – cup

41 I This is a friend of mine. (May I introduce …)
Excuse me, can you tell me how I can (could) get to the Guggenheim Museum?
Excuse me, could (can) you tell me the time?
Excuse me, could (can) you change a dollar bill? (… have you got change for a dollar bill?)
You're welcome.

41 M Excuse me, is this (that) seat taken?
It's hardly safe to walk through Central Park.
Take the subway to Columbus Circle and then walk one block and you're at the Mayflower Hotel.
Be careful when you go on the subway in New York. (Mind how you go on …)
Watch out for pickpockets!
Mind where you're going.
Have a nice day.
Thank you very much (thanks a lot) for your (all the) information and the useful (piece of) advice.
You're welcome. (That's all right.)

Unit 42

42 B Spanish settlers were the first who came to San Francisco.
They called it Yerba Buena.
Because they were looking for gold.
A terrible earthquake destroyed a large part of San Francisco.
They're living in Berkeley near San Francisco.
He's asked to play in a baseball game.

42 E Bob says he's going to Los Angeles tomorrow.
They say they're living on campus.
Tell him she's not very well today.
Jane and Russell say they're not Americans.
Tell her she's lost her map.
Tell her they're coming to tea on Sunday.
Chuck says he's studying business administration.
He says he's heard the news.

42 G He wants to know if you're tired.
He asks how old you are.
He asks if you can run fast.
He wants to know if you've got a car.
He wants to know where you live.
He asks why you're dressed like that.
He asks which university you go to.
He wants to know if you earn a good salary.
He wants to know if you like travelling.
He asks who this man is.

42 H Jane and Russell arrived in the States four weeks ago.
Carol and Chuck have known each other a long time.
He hasn't decided yet what to study.
Last week Frenchie was arrested for armed robbery.
They have been living on campus for a week.
In 1963 John F. Kennedy was killed by an assassin.
Chuck was in 12th grade last year.
Russell hasn't been to San Francisco before.
Senator Gatewater has been in Congress for twelve years.

42 I knowledge – difficulty – life – decision – marriage – meeting – difference – importance – defense (*BE:* defence) – election

42 K
campus	–	college or university grounds
grade	–	class
room-mate	–	person sharing a room
freshman	–	first year student
degree	–	academic title
cheerleader	–	crowd stimulator

42 N Which school are you going to?
Pardon me? I didn't get that.
I'd like to know what you're studying.
He says he's studying business administration.
I'd like to know where you're living.
I'd like to know if you like sport.
Thank you very much for the interview.
You're welcome.

Unit 43

43 B Because the writer of the play is coming to watch the rehearsal.
Because he's broken his arm.
He should (ought to) be playing the Ghost.
He's the author of the play they're rehearsing.
They said it was a great work of art. (They said it was good.)
Because Mary played the wrong music and Mr Benson liked it.

43 F He said he was tired.
He said the author was there that day.
She said it had been cold the day before.
He said he wanted more feeling in my lines.
He asked me to close the window.
She said she hadn't liked him.
She said the message had been handed to her the day before.
She said she couldn't help me.
He said he might need some more actors the following year.
He said he wouldn't come the next day.

43 H He asked what the play was like.
He wanted to know what had happened to the music.
She asked if (whether) Frank was directing the play.
She wanted to know if (whether) he had been playing football.
He asked who had been on the phone.
She asked if (whether) I didn't have a dictionary.
He wanted to know if (whether) I had spoken to Mr Benson.
She enquired when I would come back.
She asked how we had got on with the rehearsal.
He had no idea why he couldn't cover the story.

43 I
The play is terrible.	He left a note.
She was late.	Naturally you can't come.
We'll rehearse at once.	You haven't begun rehearsing.
Don't be silly.	I want excellent performances.

43 J They were not interested in taking part in the conference.
After long negotiations the new trade agreement was finally signed.
Those lines are not in this play.
I want first class performances from everyone.
Lauren gave Frenchie a useful piece of advice.

43 L She said she had been born in Manchester.
She said she had been brought up in London.
She said she had been studying at a drama school there for three years.
She said she'd like to act in a Shakespeare production.
Tom said he'd broken his arm.
Tom said he'd been playing cricket.
Tom said he couldn't come to rehearsal.

Unit 44

44 B In a dentist's waiting-room.
Because he's got a job to finish and he's on his own at the moment.
He should (ought to) be back by 11 o'clock.
Because they're checking the stock in his firm.
She's doing a crossword puzzle.
Because he wants to have a look at the sports page.
(Because he wants to know the football results.)
The noise of a drill.
Because she was afraid of the dreadful noise.
He was repairing his drill.

44 E I think we're being watched.
The newspaper is being printed.
When I was in New York, the Museum of Modern Art was being rebuilt.
A lot of money is being spent on nuclear weapons.
The rooms were being cleaned. (*or:* ... have just been cleaned.)
We're being forced to work overtime.
A patient is being treated.
Tea is being served.

44 G I was told to wait.
What language is spoken in Brazil?
How is it (that) spelt?
He is said to be rich.
He has never been heard of again.
I was told he had emigrated to America.
The professor wasn't listened to.
I wasn't picked up at the station.
She's supposed to be intelligent.

44 I She's been frightened away.
We'll be told the news.
She was shown round.
She was asked some questions.
The workers were promised higher wages.
He was promised a tip.
The children are told a story.
We're being taught English.
She's just been given a present.

44 K It'll be done very soon (very quickly).
We're having to check the goods available for sale.
He can't bear this any longer.
People should complain about him. (... should make a complaint about him.)

44 L Your sister's husband is your brother-in-law.
Your mother's brother is your uncle.
Your father's sister is your aunt.
Your husband's sister is your sister-in-law.
Your husband's parents are your parents-in-law.
Your sister's son is your nephew.
Your aunt's son is your cousin.
Your mother's parents are your grandparents.
You are your husband's wife.
Your son is your mother's grandson.

44 N I'd like to make an appointment to see the dentist, please.
I've got toothache.
Which tooth is giving you trouble? (… is troubling you?)
Could you give me an injection, please?
Wouldn't it be better for you to see a doctor?
(Hadn't you better see a doctor?)
I'd recommend Dr X. (I'd recommend you to go to Dr X.)
My little son is afraid of the dentist.
I'm worrying about the future.
Get well soon!

Unit 45

45 B Old Bailey
He was an English author; he wrote *Robinson Crusoe*.
When the Inns of Court originated (were founded) in the 13th century, they were places where law students lived and took their meals.
He's Russell's pupil.
Because he wanted to apologise for his bad parking.
Because he's saving up for a new car.
120 miles are 192 kilometres.

45 E He's no good at making money.
She was afraid of losing her way.
I'm tired of answering your questions.
He couldn't get accustomed to working late.
Jane's fond of dancing.
He was responsible for preparing the meeting.
Would you be interested in telling me about it?
The actors were happy about working for us.
Are you keen on travelling?

45 G I'm sure you'll soon succeed in speaking English well.
You won't have any difficulties in passing the examination.
There was no danger of losing the case.
I think he's afraid of being accused.
He can't change his habit of smoking before breakfast.
I've no reason for telling you that.
We have the pleasure of acknowledging your order.
It's no use complaining now.
I think it's no good writing to him. (I don't think it's much good writing to him.)
Excuse me interrupting you. (Excuse my interrupting you.)

45 I di**ffi**cult – **court**room – **din**ing-hall – to**geth**er – **pu**pil – **mo**ment – **mat**ter – a**pol**ogise – a**fford** – **dan**gerous – ex**pen**sive – ad**van**tage – **E**dinburgh – re**mem**ber – **some**thing – **fell**ow – down**stairs** – **per**fectly – **mor**ning – **own**er

45 J careless – fast – cheap – small – easy – public

45 L How do you mean? (What do you mean?)
What are you driving at? (What are you aiming at?)
Aren't you being a bit too hard on your children?
Could I have a word with you for a moment?
What's troubling you?
How about going to the dining-hall for a bite to eat?
I can't stand being interrupted all the time.

Unit 46

46 B Britain joined the Common Market in 1973.
Because they are dissatisfied and usually want higher wages.
He talked to a business friend. (He talked to another manager.)
She's the shop steward.
He heard his boss's telephone conversation. He heard that his boss wanted to stop the morning tea-break.
They agreed to a lightning strike.
They intend to call a general meeting.

46 H You'd better tell her yourself.
He promised to come.
I advise you to stay in bed.
I'll let you know as soon as possible.
Did anyone notice the thief leave the house?
We'd rather go home.
I saw her cross the road when the lights were red.
We asked the mail order firm to send us the catalogue.
They invited me to spend my holidays at their home.
Mr Benson watched them rehearse for the play.
He refuses to pay a higher rent.
We managed to catch the train.

46 J *Suggested acknowledgment of order*

Mr John Reed
25 Milk Street
Truro, Cornwall

6 July 19..

Dear Mr Reed

We acknowledge receipt of your order (*or:* Thank you for your order) for two sets of tea-towels. The order has been passed on to our despatch department and delivery should be made on July 14 or 15.

Yours faithfully
Jonathan Kenny Ltd.

46 N I've decided (made up my mind) to stay at home this summer.
I can't afford to go away.
I don't mind staying in town.
The cost of living is going up and incomes are going down.
You may be right on this (that) point. You may be right there.
What can we do about it?

Unit 47

47 B Cornwall is in the south-west of Britain.
Because of the influence of the Gulf Stream.
Suggested answer: Penzance, St. Ives, Polperro.
The stranger advised Russell to learn from experience and not from handbooks (manuals).
He has his car serviced every 6,000 miles.
Because Russell's letting the engine run.
He wanted to sell him his car.

47 E I'm having my car filled up.
I've seen it.
They had the thief arrested.
She didn't have the tap repaired.
You need to have your visa for America renewed.
I'll have the room painted next week. (I'm going to have …, I'm having …)
You shouldn't have that tree cut down.
She's (= She has) cleaned the suit.
She has the suit cleaned.
Have your hair cut.
Have the letter translated.
I've translated it already.

47 G Yesterday he had (*or:* he got) his car filled up at the garage.
I'll have (*or:* I'll get) the car washed tomorrow. (I'm going to have …)
Don't let me stop you.
I don't think we should have (*or:* we should get) that car towed away.
You must have (*or:* You must get) the brakes adjusted.
He makes me laugh.

47 H Much progress has been made in technology since World War II.
What are you doing the weekend after next?
He should have done his homework.
She's always making the same mistake.
Don't make that noise!
I hate doing the cooking and washing-up.
Let's get somebody to do all the boring jobs.
She's just made a cake.

47 I Don't stop. Carry on with your work.
He doesn't know much about politics.
I'm interested in learning more about cars.
Let's get rid of the bags.
We don't agree with you there.
I couldn't find out his telephone number.
She didn't believe in his ability.
They argued about the economic situation in Britain.

47 J pollution – health – poison – danger – safety – expectation – introduction – building – development – description

47 M I've decided (made up my mind) to spend my next holidays in Cornwall.
I intend (I'm intending) to look for a part-time job.
What caused you to change your mind.
I'm planning to study business administration.

Unit 48

48 B Stonehenge is in Wiltshire.
It was probably constructed 4,000 years ago.
Because he's new to the job. (Because it's his first day on the beat.)
Suggested answer: I think it was the driver of the car, because he was driving too close behind the cyclist.
Because a dog ran into the road.

48 F Da er sehr reich ist, kann sich Mr Trump eine Yacht leisten. (Da Mr Trump sehr reich ist, kann er sich …)
Nachdem (Da) sie im Fußballtoto gewonnen hatte, kaufte sich Jane ein Haus in Südfrankreich.
Da sie nicht in der Lage war, das Rad zu wechseln, bat sie einen anderen Fahrer, sie mitzunehmen.
Nachdem ich den Artikel fertiggeschrieben hatte, trank ich eine Tasse Tee.
Sie kauft niemals die Artikel, die im Fernsehen angepriesen werden. (… für die im Fernsehen geworben wird.)

Die Sprache, die in Brasilien gesprochen wird, ist Portugiesisch.
Ich hörte ein Konzert, das vom New Yorker Philharmonie-Orchester gegeben wurde.
Das junge Mädchen, das bei dem Unfall verletzt wurde, wurde ins Krankenhaus gebracht. (Das bei dem Unfall verletzte Mädchen …)

As (Because / Since) he is very rich, Mr Trump can afford a yacht. (*or:* As Mr Trump is very rich, he can afford a yacht.)
As (Because / Since) she won (= had won) the football pools, Jane bought a house in the South of France. (*or:* After she had won …)
As (Because / Since) she wasn't able (= was unable) to change the wheel, she asked another driver to give her a lift.
When (After / As soon as) I had finished the article, I had a cup of tea.
She never buys the products that (which) are advertised on television.
The language that (which) is spoken in Brazil is Portuguese.
I heard a concert that (which) was given by the New York Philharmonic Orchestra.
The young girl who (that) was injured (= had been injured) in the accident was taken to hospital.

48 G Hearing the news, I went home.
The policeman asking her about the accident was very polite.
Living in the country, they had few visits from their friends.
(While) Walking in the park, I met Jane.
(After) Having filled in the insurance form, she sent it to the insurance company straight away. (*or:* After filling in …)
You should be careful when driving beside a cyclist.
He sat in the armchair smoking a pipe.
When telephoning someone in London from abroad, just dial 1, not 01.

48 H You must be careful when crossing the street.
The car offered to me yesterday had already been sold.
Who was the man talking to you in the pub?
Being very tired, he went to bed early.
Feeling ill, he didn't want to make his speech.
Not knowing any French, he couldn't make himself understood. (Being unable to speak French …)
The people involved in the accident have given their statements.
The dentist recommended to me by a friend of mine is very good.

48 I crime   – b) drive   breaking – b) wait
incident – c) into   down   – a) noun
young   – c) hungry   details – b) to read
glad   – a) language   version – a) to earn

48 J Experienced means having practical knowledge or skill. For example: an experienced teacher.
Investigate means examine, go into (a matter).
Detect means discover or find.
A vehicle means anything that runs on wheels.
On duty means to be at work, to do a regular job.
Different means not the same as. For example: he's wearing a different suit today.

48 L I'm (so) sorry to hear (about) that.
Can I help you? (Is there anything I can do for you?)
Get well soon.
I'm looking forward to seeing you again next week.
Don't worry about your job, everything will be all right. (There's no need [for you] to worry …)
If I were you, I wouldn't come (back) to the office too early.
I'd recommend you to take a long holiday.

Unit 49

49 B Darts is a British invention.
She's from London, but she now plays for the "Royal Oak" team.
Because he's in bed with flu.
Each player usually has three darts.
One of them suggested that the "Long Hall" team should throw one dart each and the "Royal Oak" player should throw three darts.

49 E We saw a very good play at the theatre.
John played football very well last Saturday.
The film we saw last night was terribly boring.
The photographs are extremely nice.
He's a dangerous driver.
He always drives too fast.
The coffee tasted awful.
I'm awfully sorry I'm late.
He looked around carefully.
The young woman looked beautiful in her red dress.
He quickly offered us another room.
She was deeply disappointed.
They ought to play fair.
We must train hard for the next match.

49 F The players are in very good form.
We liked the evening very much.
They were very surprised to see Jane win.
Thank you very much.
I'm very sorry indeed.
I regret very much what happened.

49 H This exercise is not too bad. It's fairly easy.
I'm rather tired. Let's go.
Your car is rather slow. You should get a new one.
I want a larger car. But they're rather expensive.
He plays the trumpet fairly well, but he still needs a lot of practice.
You play rather well. Please come and play again.

49 I Have you read *David Copperfield* as well? (…, too?, Have you also read *David Copperfield*?)
She's got two dogs and a cat, too. (… and a cat as well., She's also got …)
I can't come tomorrow either.
You must (You've got to) change the sparking plugs as well.
(You must also …, You've also got to …, You must change the sparking plugs, too.)
My cousin can't swim either.

49 K I watch the programme to learn English.
He goes to the pub so that he can play darts.
We left early so as to get there on time.
Let's train hard so that we'll win next time.
She drove slowly in order to avoid an accident.

49 M Have you ever been to New York?
Wherever we went, we found the people very friendly.
Whenever he came to Paris, he always stayed at the Plaza Hotel.
Whoever you are, I'm not interested.
Whatever problems you (may) have, you can always come to me.

49 N **cham**pion – to**night** – **ter**ribly – **dif**ficult – **traf**fic jam – **mo**torway – **dif**ferent – be**gin**ner – **ac**tually – **ac**cident – sug**gest** – **mi**nute

49 O
difficult	–	easy	right	–	wrong
big	–	small	better	–	worse
late	–	early	quick	–	slow
long	–	short	a different number …	–	an equal number … (the same number …)

49 P What'll you have?
I think I'll have half a pint of bitter.
I'm terribly sorry I'm late. (I'm very sorry …, I'm so sorry …)

That's all right. (It doesn't matter., Never mind.)
Let's put the glasses somewhere else so that we don't knock them over.
It's getting rather late.
I hope Frank does come.
I'd suggest we don't wait any longer. (Let's not wait any longer.)
It's been a pleasure to talk to you. (… talking to you.)

Unit 50

50 B   "Breakfast Time" is an early morning programme of news, sport, and reports from Britain and the rest of the world.
He's rehearsing his show (programme).
He's expecting news about the strike in the Midlands.
Because he had money on the favourite horse.
He was eating his breakfast.

50 E   After studying at Berkeley, he became a lawyer. (After having studied …)
Will you get my breakfast while I discuss the show with the producer? (no ing-form!)
You should fasten your seat belts when driving.
Not knowing what to do, I telephoned him.
Having forgotten my wallet, I had to go home to get it.
Being so tall, he drives a large car.
Her mother being ill, she couldn't leave the house. (= With her mother being ill, …)
Having no small change, he couldn't phone home.

50 F   We saw them climbing (up) the mountain.
Did you hear us talking Welsh?
I watched him go into the house.
I heard him going down the stairs.

50 G   The satellite pictures just coming in show a low approaching from the Atlantic.
But I expect today's meeting will be cancelled.
I broke my arm when practising a new exercise.
Our viewers don't just want to see commercials while eating breakfast.
I don't like to be interrupted while rehearsing my show.
If we don't improve the show soon, there won't be any people watching it. (There won't be any people watching the show if we don't improve it soon.)
He's just destroyed the kitchen, trying out his new gas cooker.

50 H   Gilbert, an old friend of Humphrey's, had been living (lived / had lived) in Cornwall for many years before he returned to London.
By the end of next year you'll have finished your studies.
He would enjoy the concert if he were here.
The police found Billy last night. He had run away from home two days before.
You'll miss the train if you don't hurry.
If I were in your position, I would act differently.
I've just received a letter from Jane.
He came to see me this morning.
She hasn't finished work yet.
What did you buy yesterday?
When did you lose your trumpet?
I haven't seen him for three years.

50 I A producer is a person who (that) is responsible for the production of a television or a radio programme.
A correspondent is a person who contributes reports to a radio or television programme.
Viewing figures give the number of people watching television at a given time.
A roving reporter is a correspondent who travels around.
Sub-titles are translated captions to a film.
Commercials are advertisements on radio or television.

50 J news – interrupted – viewers – strike – destroyed – cancelled – approaching – climb – hurry up – situated – presenter – menu

50 M I like (enjoy) watching television in the evenings.
I wish there was (were) always something in the news to cheer people up.
I'm disappointed to hear that news.
I haven't had (received) any report from my colleague today.
He might have had a breakdown. (... could have had ...)
There won't be any newspapers tomorrow because the editors are on strike.

Unit 51

51 B They're visiting a car factory.
He's the Chief Designer of the car factory.
Because he was waiting for a new robot.
It was injured in an accident.
Suggested answer: It can be programmed, it doesn't get tired, it doesn't ask for more money, it can't be injured, it doesn't go on strike, it doesn't come in late.
He was replaced by the robot he was waiting for.
Henry Ford
Because they're worried that the machines might take away their jobs.

51 E They shouldn't be allowed to smoke.
The cars can't be tested.
The tyres have been bought from a different factory.
The car was being driven by a careless driver.
You'll be invited to visit our factory.
The information was being processed.
This matter must be looked into.
He was told to be quick.
In the early days cars were made like carriages.
Only one job was done by each worker at one stage of production.
Mistakes are made by human beings, not by robots.
Your wallet has been found.
He's being sent abroad.
You'll be looked after.
Something must be done (has to be done) for the poor.
Football is played all over the world.

51 F Last year he spent two weeks in the USA. All his expenses were paid by his firm.
Brooklyn Bridge was designed by a German architect.
In 1982 the Barbican Centre was officially opened by Queen Elizabeth II.
The Sears Tower in Chicago is said to be the tallest skyscraper in the world.
My car was towed away yesterday.
Any car causing an obstruction can be towed away by the police.
Jane and Russell travelled to Munich by plane. They were picked up at the airport by car.
During the conference Senator Gatewater was interrupted several times by his secretary.
David Copperfield was written by Charles Dickens.
That bridge will have been built by next Christmas.

51 G The assembly work is done here. All the parts are put together.
Do you think robots can be relied on?
He was taken no notice of.
The doctor was sent for.
She has never been heard of again.
This statement has been objected to.
What is he being accused of?
The problem ought to be dealt with next time.
The forms have to be filled in.
He was run over by a car.

51 I A robot is a machine that does the work formerly done by men.
An error is a mistake.
To assemble cars means to put them together.
A chance is an opportunity.
To visit means to come and see.
Efficient here means capable.
To increase means to grow or to raise.

51 J Menschlicher Irrtum ausgeschlossen

Letzte Woche gab man mir die (= hatte ich) Gelegenheit, die Autofabrik von „UK Motors" zu besichtigen. Es ist erstaunlich, wie sich die Produktionsmethoden verändert haben, seit die ersten Roboter eingeführt wurden. Sie werden immer zuverlässiger und leistungsfähiger. Roboter werden nicht nur für die Montage, sondern auch zur Überprüfung und Kontrolle der Autos eingesetzt. Selbst wenn die Autos getestet werden, werden sie von einem Roboter gefahren.
Die Betriebsleiter sind (*oder:* Die Geschäftsleitung ist) natürlich für die Roboter, weil sie nicht zu spät kommen, nicht müde werden, nicht verletzt werden können, nicht krank werden können und keine höheren Löhne fordern. Sie erwarten (*oder:* Sie erwartet), daß die Roboter die industrielle Produktion erhöhen.
Diese elektronischen Arbeiter sind dabei, die Gesellschaft völlig zu verwandeln.

51 K A letter to Constance Smile,
Public Relations Officer of UK Motors factory

Dear Mrs Smile

I'm writing to thank you for giving me an opportunity to visit your factory. I was very impressed by your robots. It is amazing what these machines can do. I do hope, however, that workers who are replaced by robots will be offered retraining for other work.

Thank you again for all the information you gave me.

Yours sincerely
Jane Egan

51 L Are the car bodies made here?
The car bodies are bought ready-made from a firm in Sheffield.
Are the cars being assembled here?
All the assembly work is done here in this workshop.
Are the cars painted here?
Several coats of paint are applied.
Where are the cars tested?
The cars are tested by robots.
How many cars are produced here a week?
About 500, one third of them is sold in Britain, two thirds are exported.